New Jungle, Same Old Monkeys

My Missionary Meanderings

New Jungle, Same Old Monkeys

My Missionary Meanderings

By Margaret Anne Lawson
with Dayspring MacLeod

RoperPenberthy

RoperPenberthy
Freedom Publishing LLP
Grieves Cottage, Drumelzier Haugh Farm
Broughton, Biggar
ML12 6JD

British Library Cataloguing in Publication Data
A catalogue record for this book is available from the
British Library

ISBN: 978-1-908154-30-9

Cover design by Esther Kotecha
Typeset by Avocet Typeset, Somerton, Somerset, TA11 6RT
Printed and bound by Nørhaven

TABLE OF CONTENTS

CHAPTER 1

THE LONG AND WINDING ROAD

My story could have started in my early teens at the boarding school I attended near Windermere. It was a happy time in my life where a small but enthusiastic group of Christian pupils met nightly in a dormitory. I started going along and said the 'Sinners' Prayer', asking Jesus into my life and accepting the forgiveness of my sins, and I felt something exciting and wonderful happen inside.

Every Sunday evening Miss Gunning, a Christian teacher, arranged for us to be presented with a good cause that we could support with our weekly giving. One week, Jim Glazebrook, a war hero whose story is told in his book *Someone to Watch Over Me*, came to tell us about Mission Aviation Fellowship. MAF was started by Christian pilots who flew in the Second World War and who wanted to use their skills to save lives instead of taking lives. They operate in rural areas where there is often no other form of transport for missionaries and vital medical services to get to people. Jim showed us a film of the true story of MAF pilots and evangelists Nate Saint and Jim Elliot, who were speared to death on a riverbank in South America by Auca Indians. Their wives had returned to the Aucas with forgiveness which broke down barriers and led to many committing themselves to God. It is an incredible story and it could have filled me with an inextinguishable fire to serve God, drawing a straight line from that day to my eventual missionary service. But, in fact, few of the lines in my life have ever been straight!

Although I had made a profession of faith, I didn't really grasp the meaning of what being a Christian was about, and when the time came for the older girls to leave, I was left in charge of the group. I wasn't ready for that responsibility and made little of it. Feeling a failure, I also felt hurt and ashamed.

One sunny day when I was 16, and when I was supposed to be walking to class, I stopped and stood still. I was alone. The smell of flowering azaleas was fragrant in my nostrils and I could hear the background sound of water trickling into a fern-lined pool. In the midst of this Eden, I did as Eve before me and told God to get lost. I felt something of His sorrow, but the stubborn adolescent in me was relentless. It was the worst decision of my life! Nothing happened immediately, however; imperceptibly, and slowly but surely, my life started on a downward spiral which would not be reversed until ten years and many sorrows later.

That seemingly happy 16-year-old thrived throughout school, and was voted Head Girl. However, the demands of that position led to a steep decline in my test results, and rather than the glowing studies in Veterinary Medicine that I had envisioned, I ended up in a less desirable Zoology course at the University of Aberdeen. There I built up a fine history of boyfriends, one-night stands, academic failure, alcoholism, and, apparently, nation-wide notoriety! On one occasion a young chap in an Edinburgh pub was telling me stories of a wild woman he'd heard of up at the University of Aberdeen, a woman with a legendary lack of boundaries. It dawned on me that he was speaking about me but I was so far gone that I just laughed!

In my first term in university I read three reports in national newspapers warning of the dangers of heavy drinking. I was already drinking more in one day than they said was acceptable for a week and, at its worst, doing so 9 nights out of every 10. I thought what wimps those people were who believed this stuff;

unlike others, I could handle it! I wasn't close enough to any one person for anyone to know how bad things were. I often drove my car when entirely drunk. I would give my keys to a trusted friend and then be able to appeal for them back at the end of the evening, appearing quite sober.

Many times, I would wake up thinking I hadn't done anything reprehensible and breathe a sigh of relief only to be informed later (often by people I couldn't remember) of the amusing, and not so amusing, things I had said and done whilst under the influence. I laughed it off and carried on. I made a noise loudly in public – 'woop, woop, woop' – the 'mating call of the lesser spotted U-boat,' I said. People certainly knew when I was around!

The inside of my mind was a busy place. In my sober moments I would decide on things that I would not do or say; however, after a few drinks and prompted by other voices in my head, I would at some point do and say those very things. In my reckoning there were two sorts of people; those who were boring and didn't have the guts to do the wild things I got up to and those who were contemptible because they did some or all of the things I thought that I would never do. The former grew in number and the latter decreased. It was a life of shifting goalposts – and it was as if the voices in my head went right for the new 'line'. With each major compromise these voices increased in number and volume, always succeeding in persuading me to do many things I had sworn I never would. At first any increase felt uncomfortable and required a recalibration. My spiritual skin felt stretched, but these 'presences' made room for themselves, and for the others who were later to join them.

I only got a BSc (Hons) 2:2, but I didn't deserve even that and I knew it. I had wasted my university career in drunkenness and loose living and I decided not to go to the graduation. Mum asked me one day over the summer, 'When is your graduation?' I took some pleasure in informing her 'Today!' She was, of course, hugely disappointed.

Still in Aberdeen, I took a postgraduate course in Corrosion Engineering. Whilst there, in the habit of doing the minimum coursework necessary to placate the uni lecturers, it was a shock to have to turn up to all classes and complete work on time! I got so completely plastered at the first end-of-term bash with the lecturers that I groped the course organiser's bottom and fell over in a pile of shoes in front of his wife! They were all amazed that I turned up for the next term – and without apparent embarrassment. I could go on and on with these stories.

Thankfully, my story doesn't start in Aberdeen either!

After university, I lived in a rented cottage in Aberdeenshire with my boyfriend, Julian, and during the week I lived in Nottingham, working for an engineering company called Stanton Ironworks. Even when Julian and I were living together, I sometimes went out and on occasion got off with someone; not all the way, but it was a definite sign of my lack of self-control and commitment. Every time I did it, the unknowing Julian would come home with a really nice present for me. What resulted was a museum of reminders of how bad I was. It was a relief to get away from it.

We had tranquil countryside weekends – but then I would leave with more of my possessions on the Sunday afternoon. Every time I removed something else Julian felt more abandoned. He wasn't wrong, I was moving on, not just from life in Aberdeen but also life with him. I bought a house near work. I was on a confusing and troubling spiritual journey.

Julian couldn't bear the increasing distance between us and asked me to marry him. I said yes, but even though I loved the ring he'd bought, I didn't like wearing it. Once again, after a short time of excitement, I felt the disappointment of even this not making me happy. Why couldn't I be like other people who seemed content with car, career, home ownership and marriage? Three miserable months, and much soul-searching later, I phoned Julian and broke it off. He was hurt and I was still deeply unhappy. We met up a few times but I could not relent;

the relationship was scarred by my infidelities and discontent and I couldn't go back. He would not take back the lovely engagement ring and his mother told people that I had only got engaged to get the ring. Julian didn't bother to disillusion her.

My Nana was as horrified as if I had divorced and in those days divorce (especially in Galloway, a region in the southwest corner of Scotland, where I grew up) was almost unheard of. It was considered a troubling event, not just for the family but for the society around them too, and our family were supposed to be better than that. I had brought irreparable shame on a respectable family. In years to come two of my cousins followed suit and Nana remarked, 'This family is full of broken engagements!'

But even that is not my real story. That's just my past!

My real story begins in the back garden of my Nottingham house. One evening, while letting my dog Lucy out before bedtime, I had a feeling that there was a monster behind the bins. I called Lucy and slammed and locked the back door behind us, panting with fear. As a teenager, with the spiritual vacuum in my soul left by my rejection of God screaming to be filled, I had made up a prayer to the devil, inviting him into my life and hoping for a horned, goat-hoofed apparition at the end of my bed. There was no apparition and, if there had been, it would have no doubt driven me back to God. Knowing this, the enemy of our souls moved in cautiously and gently at first until he could be sure of me being so corrupted as to be unable to stand against him, and I was now at that point.

I closed myself in my bedroom and searched for some distraction to take away my fear. An avid reader with no TV, I had run out of books to read in the house. All I had left was John Bunyan's classic allegory 'Pilgrim's Progress' and a Christian book about spiritual things written by the American evangelist David Wilkerson. While reading at 2 a.m. I was overcome by the impression of something evil lurking outside my bedroom door. I was terrified and wanted to call Nash, one of the two Christians at work. However, I wasn't about to go out of the bedroom, much less to the phone box; and of course, how could I bother Nash at that time in the early hours of the morning? The next evening, who should appear at the door but Nash himself. I told him what had happened, and he said, 'If it was me I would walk towards whatever it is and command it to go in the name of Jesus!' It sounded a bit daft to me, but that night in the garden the same fear came, and I did what he had suggested. It was like switching a light on in a dark room; the fear went instantly, and made me think that there might be more to this Jesus thing than I had thought.

Although work was a happy place, I myself was far from happy. I drank less often, but when I did drink, I might or might not be able to stop and when I couldn't, my behaviour was increasingly outrageous and always in front of people who would gossip. The wheedling voices in my head played cat and mouse with me. I would be okay for a time and start to imagine that the problem was gone. Then, just when I was starting to feel good – bam, yet another drunken indiscretion. It wore me down to the point where, eventually, I realised I was never going to be in control again. I had done all I could do! If people didn't look at me too closely it would appear that my life was going well but, with my drink problem, my increasing fear of the spiritual world and my deep dissatisfaction with what 'normal' life had to offer, I was in despair.

People have different triggers to make them feel that life is actually unbearable. It may be bad relationships, loneliness, physical pain or a myriad of other things. For me, it was the hopelessness of my slavery to sin. On April Fools' Day in 1989 I went to a party with workmates and got exceedingly drunk and the way I behaved shocked even myself. Rather than describing a situation which I have now finally let go, I'll ask you to remember the time at which you were the most ashamed of yourself. Add to that the shame you would feel on doing the worst thing you can imagine, something far outside your own boundaries, and you'll have an idea how I felt. I despised myself.

This was my lowest point and, while I outwardly maintained a cheerful and upbeat image, I formed a plan to kill myself.

I knew that if God was real – and reading the Bible for the first time in a decade, I was starting to realise He was – He would send me to hell and I deserved it! I had often joked about hell being a fun place to meet up with your wildest mates, but now I remembered the horror movies I'd watched as a child, the ones that had made me tiptoe up the stairs nearly paralysed with fear, and hell sounded like being trapped in one of those movies for all eternity. I read verses in the Gospels about Jesus judging people after they died and sending them to a place where the flames never went out – and I knew I was on my way there.

One night I poured myself a favourite tipple and, looking into the glass, I found that I couldn't see to the bottom of it – it was like a deep, dark hole. It gave me the same feeling I'd had in the garden, of a malevolent presence lying in wait, and I knew that if I drank what was in that glass, that would be it for me. With a shiver, I threw it away, but I knew the forces that controlled my life were closing in on me.

During this time, the other Christian at work, Kenny, had left Stanton and was getting married to his long-term girlfriend Marcia. Nash and I were invited to their wedding and we travelled to London in the same car. It was a vibrant, colourful and noisy African affair and it was the first truly Christian wedding I had ever been to. They made promises to each other, conscious of the presence of the God that they knew personally.

At the reception Kenny came to talk to me. 'Are you a Christian yet?' he asked.

'I can't seem to get off the fence!' I replied gaily.

'Wait and I will send someone to speak to you.'

One of the ushers came over and we talked. I was my usual cocky smiling self. He said to me, 'You need to hear from God. I have the strongest feeling that you need to cry!'

The effect these words had on me was like walking into a brick wall. It was true, I had been choked up with tears for days and hadn't realised my need to cry, until he said those words.

'I'd like to pray with you,' he said. I agreed and off he went for a few moments.

He came back with the bride and groom and we went into a room at the side of the hall. They started to pray and I started to cry, and I cried and cried. I curled up in a ball on the floor and, as they continued to pray, one of them asked me to stand and the tears dried up.

I heard the words: 'Open your mouth and say whatever comes out.' A series of strange words came out. It was what Christians call speaking in tongues (this is a language someone has never learned and is given by God as a gift to help us in many different ways in our relationship with Him). For some, this is a controversial topic, but this was not the case for me. It just came naturally and I felt different inside.

On the way home Nash invited me to come to his church the next morning. 'If you don't like it,' he said, 'you can find somewhere else that suits you.'

The next morning, he picked me up and we went along to the Christian Centre, or T Street, which was renting the Albert Hall in Nottingham for morning services. About 1,500 people came regularly and the church's own building was not big enough to hold the congregation. It wasn't the traditional church service that I had been used to in younger years, but I felt that I had come home. I still feel most 'at home' there, even today when I live a long way away.

One of my first Sundays at church, a lady I was chatting with suddenly said to me 'One day you'll be a missionary!' I went along with it, but I can't say that I actually knew what a missionary was at that time!

What had caused me to reject God at 16 was ignorance of what true Christianity is. I'd thought I was recruiting God to serve me, rather than the other way around, so I felt betrayed every time another disappointment came along. This time I was on a steep learning curve, starting to realise that I was now His servant, and I had a pressing hunger to learn. The only book I read for the next three years was the Bible. So much of it spoke to my spirit and I fed on it. I went to every church service and every prayer meeting I could and I joined a midweek home group – a small gathering for getting to know a few people better and studying the Bible more intimately. I served wherever I could, usually washing up after the obligatory cups of tea and coffee at church events.

The Bible says that we must – figuratively speaking, but nevertheless consciously – be 'crucified with Christ'; this means that that the life we now live is not of ourselves, but Christ living in us. It was as if my suicide plan had really happened – in that the old me, defeated and dogged by sin, was dead. Everything that happened from now on was me as a new person, writing on a clean slate with a new motivation and a new standard. As I was a newborn in the faith, my mission was now finding out what God wanted of me and how I was to live.

CHAPTER 2

SCOTTISH THISTLE

One of the first indications that I had been changed was in a small detail of life. An example of this was that I bought expensive Laura Ashley wallpaper for my sitting room; the pattern was named 'Scottish Thistle'. A Christian friend of a friend was setting up in business for himself and needed work and so I asked him to paper the room. I got home to discover that the chap had hung the wallpaper upside down! Being a very particular person, it bothered me but he had already papered over half the room and if I asked him to rectify it the cost would have been pretty significant. I woke in the middle of the night, when things can assume a greater intensity and importance, and I started fuming. However, I felt God asking me not to insist on my own way but to be deliberately merciful to this man at a time when he was short of money and not to even mention the mistake to him, which would have hurt him, but rather to totally let it go. As God is God and I am His servant, I decided to obey and immediately the anger left.

On another occasion, on a Wednesday night in hard winter, I heard a car alarm. 'Oh Lord, may the thief not be successful,' went through my mind. Then I thought, 'Why am I asking God to do something when I should do what I can?' Consequently, I got out of bed, rubbed a hole in the ice on the bedroom window and looked out. All seemed okay, so I got back into bed, but I felt God asking me to get up to pray. I was tired, so made the excuse, 'The spirit is willing but the flesh is weak!'

I felt God's reply, 'Your spirit isn't even willing.' Instantly conjunctivitis, which I had previously experienced, returned and I knew that, unless I got up and prayed, there would be no healing. The background to this is that, a few weeks earlier, I had got conjunctivitis the night before heading for a big important meeting in London on behalf of my boss. At home in the evening I prayed, 'Lord, keep my eye comfortable until I can get to a chemist.' He did this but my eye was red and tender the next day and, whilst on the train, I realised that I didn't have time to get to a chemist before the meeting. I prayed for complete healing and I was healed instantly there on the train.

Back to the Wednesday night when I had felt compelled to pray. I got up and went downstairs, put on the gas heater in the dining room, and opened my Bible in Job where it talks about someone with distress in their bones and their life ebbing away and an angel being sent so that the light of life shines on them and they are saved. I felt this was for my Grandma Lawson. After an hour of prayer my eye was healed and I was free to go back to bed and, as I nestled back onto my pillow, I prayed to God, saying, 'Although I have no right to ask, please God, let me know that this hasn't just been a figment of my imagination.' On the Friday I had a call at work from Mum. On Wednesday Grandma had fallen and broken her hip and was hospitalised but Dad didn't want me coming home to see her, worried that she would think we were there to watch her die. When I got home I went back to the verses from Job and prayed that an angel (either a nurse ministering according to God's will, or a heavenly being) would visit her and I had the greatest sense of peace. She died that night with no relatives nearby. But God was there for her and I believe she has gone to be with God.

After one morning church service, I looked across the entrance hall of the church as people were leaving and saw an attractive face. I started to speak to the lady, Pat, whom it turned out lived just a short distance from my home. She invited me round, but experience from my previous lifestyle had taught me that people are quick to invite you round but don't necessarily appreciate you taking them up on the offer. So I didn't. However, a short time later, I went to a prayer meeting where we were to be divided up into triplets that would meet to pray between the bigger meetings. I stood up when those who needed a group were asked to do so and my eye caught Pat's. 'Sit down,' she mouthed, and there began a partnership of three years.

Pat taught me how to pray, how to hear God's voice amidst the clamour of voices in our lives and about mission work. She was on a Missions Course at the time and often discussed with me what she was learning and, as an experienced Christian, she taught me also to question things. I would tell her week by week what I felt God had been saying to me. 'He said the exact opposite thing to you last week!' she would point out. 'Which is it?' Pat would also insist that I judge whatever I had 'heard' from God in the light of His Word. Any personal revelations or intuitions I had must be subject to the Bible. In this way Pat trained me in the gift of discernment.

Above all, Pat taught me about praying in faith. She had become a widow in her thirties with four small children. Money had been short but God had always provided what she needed just when she needed it. Pat said to me, 'If my earthly husband, Derek, was here he wouldn't have me going to the neighbours saying he was keeping me short – that would be shameful. God is now my husband and I am not going around telling people He isn't providing for me!'

This really touched me and it was a principle that I have lived by ever since. When I gave up paid employment to follow the call of God, I did my best to use my resources wisely and to work hard at anything that was put before me. Other than that, I said to God, 'I am looking to you to provide whatever I need. I don't want to ask anyone else for anything.' And God always provided faithfully without me advertising any needs. I consider

Pat to be the spiritual mother, given by God, which my natural mother could not be to me.

Since rejecting God at 16 and becoming that 'trouble magnet', I had thought, said and done many regrettable things. I had done every wrong thing that had presented itself to me. I had messed up. God's way of putting things right is not to just let you off the hook and, nearly every day, the Holy Spirit would flag up a past misdemeanour and ask me to look at it. Inwardly I would be squirming and unwilling to relive the pain and embarrassment, but I stuck my spiritual hand in His and, in the light of His love and forgiveness, I was able to tease out the issues, always learning to clear out the rubbish.

I forgave people who had hurt me and I asked God's forgiveness for the wrongs I had done, and, when prompted by Him, with great nervousness, I traced old friends and acquaintances to ask for their forgiveness. Graciously, they forgave. It was important when tackling these things to make sure:

a) They were done solely for the benefit of the ones I had wronged and not as an emotional dumping exercise to make me feel better as I realised that sometimes it was kinder to let sleeping dogs lie. I relied on God's guidance to know when to act or not.
b) That the apology was appropriate in form to the original misdemeanour, recognising that some things are easier to put right than others.

I can remember asking Him, 'Will there ever come a time when I am not dealing with the past? Will I ever be normal?' I purposefully went around my house and asked if there were things I shouldn't have. I returned stolen goods to the Stanton offices. The other employees didn't understand why as it was standard practice to take superfluous items home. I threw out music, photos and books that might take me back to my old life. It seemed I was always giving up something, but it felt right.

After three years the daily reminder of past sins petered out and I was left to deal only with any current issues.

It's good to keep short accounts, to live life with no regrets; and I learned that guilt is only useful when it prompts one to think carefully and to put right what needs to be put right. If guilt remains after that, it is destructive. The secret is to give it to Jesus, who died that we might not only be put right before God but also that we might live with lightness of spirit.

I was called to a new standard. I was to see myself only in the light of Jesus, who lived a perfectly sinless life. There was no more room for me to excuse *any* unworthy behaviour and as such, now that my dissolute past was behind me, I started to feel convicted about more ordinary, day-to-day sinful habits – ones that many Christians will struggle with.

For instance, since school days, my relationship with food had always been fraught. While I had struggled only briefly with bulimia, my ongoing gluttony was a long-term problem. Overindulgence and regret were a vicious cycle, and this love-hate relationship with food became more intense after I came back to God. I prayed, and I tried to control my eating, but all to no avail. Eventually I gave up. Then one day I just felt that He had done something inside me and I was released.

Then there was the speeding issue. Many Galloway drivers did not obey speed limits. Nana, my Father, all of us young ones – we never stuck to them. I had made a conscious decision that the speed limits didn't apply to me and had driven accordingly. But now I wanted to do the right thing. The strange thing was that, try as I might, in a 30 mph zone my foot would depress the accelerator and I would be at 40 mph without wanting to be; in a 60 mph zone I would be at 70 mph and so on. I tried, failed, prayed, tried again, failed and gave up. Again, this may seem to be a minor issue to many but I was determined that no sin should have control of me. A few months later, as the bells of the New Year rang out, I had a feeling that God was returning control to me again and, for the first time, I was now able to stick to speed limits – although I confess that I enjoy driving *at* the limits!

In this way, I learned what it meant to be 'free from sin'. Throughout the New Testament, we are promised that God's children are free from sin – not *will* be free, but *are* free. We will always struggle with sin during this life but, when we know God, we always have the power to resist.

Nash went to India to explore his roots and he asked me to look after a box of books. The box sat on my bedroom floor for weeks before I had a peek. The one book that caught my attention was about exorcism. Like scandal in newspapers, it had its attraction. I started to read and it was another 'bashing into a brick wall' experience! The accounts of demon possession were like reading about myself when I was out of control of my life. I suddenly realised that the inside of my head had been quiet since Kenny and Marcia's wedding. No more wheedling voices and, just as miraculously, I no longer had a drink problem. There had been no withdrawal, no temptation – I hadn't even realised I was healed! Thankfulness welled up inside me. God had taken the problem that I couldn't solve myself. After I realised what God had done so that I could have peace again, I knelt and said to Him, 'I know that I can't pay you back, but if there is anything I can do to say thank you, please tell me'. And, thinking about all the stupid risks I had taken for the pleasures of this world, I naively added, 'Send me somewhere dangerous and exciting!'

If my prayer was rash, I meant every word of it, for good. I had found, like a gift, the utter gratefulness to God which is the only true motivation for serving Him. I watched carefully for any indication of what He would have me do.

The first development was that I was promoted at work. Stanton had been great and I was due a six-monthly review with the Directors and, having just come back to faith, I prayed that God would put me in the company wherever he wanted. I also asked Him to help me not to open my big mouth and get in the way!

Despite this, I heard myself saying to the Directors that I needed to be moved to a more challenging position. 'How long do we have?' they asked. 'Six months!' I blurted out. When I came out of the meeting I thought to myself, 'Well, now you've really done it! If they don't offer a move within six months, you'll have to leave!'

Within two months I was interviewed and offered a job in the Technical Services Department. However, before I took up the job, a new chap who had been taken on as a manager was moved on and, without so much as an interview, I was put in his role. It was a meteoric rise that everyone within the company saw. However, it wasn't popular with the seven men who were used to having no manager and having free rein to do as they pleased! Untangling the inefficient ways of working that they had developed was tricky. Also, the secretary didn't like having another woman around and would come into the office and rile the men up against me. I prayed, 'Change her or move her.' She got pregnant and left to embrace long-awaited motherhood.

But I worked hard. The guys complained that they needed re-grading and pay rises and I fought for them and got what they had failed to obtain for years. However, the manager is always at fault and what I achieved was criticised and unappreciated until many years later, after I had moved on, when we met up and they thanked me.

One day I had to write a report about a pipeline failure. My boss, Geoff, called me to his office. 'If you tell the water company what's in this report, it'll cost us a lot of money,' he said, and came up with an alternative of what I should tell them. I looked at my conscience and said, 'But that's a lie. I'm a Christian. If you let me speak to the customer I will tell them the truth. Otherwise speak to them yourself!' Had I been a man, I think he would have fired me, but my God-given boldness overwhelmed him. He let me send the report to the customer and we never heard any more about it. It was a good lesson for later life – not being afraid to stand up for what is right, even if it might potentially cost a great deal.

I was still seeking God's will and did what I could at church. While I was in a position of power at work, I often spent evenings washing coffee mugs after an event! I didn't find this demeaning; my church taught new Christians the attitude that we were to serve others, not because of our gender or our inexperience, but because we were following Christ's model of lowly service. It was part of developing His character in ourselves.

However, I did have a thirst to do more – not just to serve in these small, part-time ways, but to lay my whole life at the feet of the One who had saved me from despair. I went to meetings where anyone willing to be sent somewhere by God was asked to stand up as a public statement of availability, and I stood up. I attended a World Horizons-organised open day called 'Dirty Hands', where various opportunities for Christian work were showcased. But there was nothing there for me. Then, one Saturday, I was going through the paperwork in my grandmother's old writing desk and, as I did so, I was asking God to tell me what to do. In my hand I had a booklet that had been keeping the lid from closing and, as I opened it, my eye caught an advert. 'Why not train to be an aircraft engineer for MAF?' Something inside me said, 'You could do that,' and yet another something thought it was the silliest idea I'd ever heard of – but I would walk toward the opportunity and, if it was God's plan, then He would open doors. I took the brochure to my pastor, and he told me to find out more about it. At least he didn't say it was the silliest idea *he'd* ever heard of.

At our church, there were 14 full-time pastors. None of their wives went out to work, but instead very ably supported their husbands. There were, as a result, expectations of what roles women should take. Hospitality, motherhood, and praying loomed large. Aircraft mechanic was not one of them. With this precedent, I was expecting that the leaders would not be supportive, but I couldn't have been more wrong. They were wonderfully enthusiastic and encouraging as well as wise.

I also realised that if I was going to be open about where the

Lord would send me, I had to be flexible with my diet. Because of my love of animals, I'd been a strict vegan for several years, but a missionary in rural South America or India would not have the luxury of checking sweetie packets to make sure there was no animal gelatine included – I'd have to be willing to partake of whatever hospitality people provided. I never stopped preferring vegan food, but over the next few years I was called upon to eat things I'd never dreamed of.

It was around this time I went to speak to my boss Geoff about work-related matters. As I entered his office he said to me, 'You're nearly 30. It's about time you decided what you want to do with the rest of your life. Are you going to settle down and have a family, or…?' I hardly knew what to say, and when I mentioned it to him some time later, he had no recollection whatsoever of saying it. It was so out of context and character that I took it as a confirmation from God, who can speak in any way and through anyone that He chooses.

It also came at a time when many old Stanton staff were remembering my meteoric rise from humble beginnings to potential Directorship. I had a memorable interview with the full panel of Directors to discuss my future. It was opened by the Personnel Director asking, 'So are you going to stay at Stanton or go off to run a kibbutz or something?' What could I say? He was probably being funny, but he had wandered surprisingly close to the truth!

I had to tell them about my application to MAF. Jaws hit the desk and they warned me, 'If you really mean this, then you could be made redundant at any time.' But I had to be truthful and I stuck to my story. It was a short meeting and, a few minutes after it ended, my Director, Jim Morrison, called me and said, 'Look, we understand that youngsters can be impetuous. If this is the case, then just let me know and it will be as if you never said anything about leaving.' In my head I turned away from such an idea. But it was nice to be assured of their confidence in my potential, and I was somewhat shocked to be considered so youthful that I was prone to rash resolutions, as if I had just been telling them I was planning a gap year! Perhaps it was because I was a woman entering the last decade of her prime child-bearing years, or perhaps they sensed God starting a particular engine in my heels, but everyone around me seemed to know I was at a turning point.

As it happened, I didn't make that call to Jim. Instead my application to MAF was accepted and I attended interviews and meetings to find out what I needed to do. I had to complete my mechanic's training and find the finances to do so.

It was a road that led me back to Jim Glazebrook, who had given a Sunday talk at my school about MAF. He and his wife Betty were an amazing support to me. Adopting me as a daughter they'd never had, they were endlessly kind and proud of my achievements. It's tempting to wish I could have found that relationship and life's calling back when I'd first met him as a teenager, as I would have missed a great deal of heartache and caused a great deal less too. However, the Bible tells us that 'the one who is forgiven much loves much.' That could be a summary of my Christian life and service. Perhaps if I had never fallen so far, I never would have been filled with this grateful longing to serve.

If my spiritual life was full of momentum and excitement, I may not have been immune from the desire for a normal, safe and contented life. I was often nervous and anxious, and one beautiful summer's evening, while walking the dogs through a lovely field, I burst into tears. 'Lord, why can't I be like other people? Why can't I be happy with a house and a job like other people seem to be?' I felt very sorry for myself. The reply came, 'If you want that, it's not too late; you can call Jim and say you want to keep your job.' Then I realised I didn't want that at all – I'd be bored. I realised that I owned this decision and that I *was* doing what I wanted to do, and I didn't feel hard done by anymore.

CHAPTER 3

THE OTHER CHILD

Like many new Christians, I was outspoken on the topic of my faith and had very black and white opinions. My parents weren't pleased with this latest development in my life and, rather than being supportive, they were suspicious and critical. I had hidden most of my struggles from them, so they didn't appreciate the miracle that had happened.

I had learned over the years that, if I told them the truth about a crisis I was going through, Dad would blow his top and say hurtful things and Mum would wallow in self-pity, moaning, 'I've been such a bad mother,' or 'What did I do to deserve a daughter like this?' Because of this, I had become secretive and they didn't know how completely I had disgraced myself, or how close I had come to choosing death. They were shocked by seeing my new life but there was a reason why they had turned against a life of faith. I was my parents' only child, but not their eldest child. There were two photos on my parents' wall; me, and another child, hardly more than a baby. When I asked my mother who it was, she unforthcomingly replied, 'A little boy.' It was the first indication of the sense of secrecy borne by my family. I was about ten years old before I discovered the truth about the picture that hung next to mine. My grandmother had let something slip in front of me and my closest cousin, Jane, and finally I learned about my elder brother.

Gavin, who was nearly three, used to follow Mum out back when she went to hang the washing up on the line across the farmyard. She had assumed that he was behind her, missed him for a minute, and in that short time he found some machinery. A tractor was being used to drive a sawmill. Gavin got caught in the belt between the tractor and the mill and went in up to his neck. One of the people involved in the sawing brought him to the door. The GP came from Wigtown, and while Mum sat in the kitchen blaming herself, Dad and the doctor tried to save his life. It wasn't possible to move him to hospital and he quickly passed away. The doctor said it was a blessing as he would have had many problems as a result of his injuries. It was only when sorting through my parents' possessions after their passing that I found the yellowing sheet of newspaper from the Galloway Gazette that gave some more detail.

It was obviously an event that changed our family. They had all been regular churchgoers, but grief stepped in the way of faith. They couldn't reconcile their ongoing despair with any joy found in the church and Dad often brought up the fact that farmers paid compulsory tithes to the church, and he was very quick to see and take offence at the many other faults to be commonly found in churches. He wanted nothing more to do with it all. How could a loving God let this happen to his beloved two-year-old son?

Dad was a larger-than-life character, proficient in every manly pursuit like farming, shooting, fishing on an international scale, fixing and building things, even racing-car driving. He always had a current project that he obsessed about until he had conquered the challenges that would have caused others to give up. And Dad assumed Mum and I wanted to hear all about it, so all mealtimes were either Mum's ongoing lecture on table manners ('All joints on the table will be carved') or Dad's latest obsession. Sheep-shearing was perhaps the longest. We lived and breathed sheep and shearing for many years. Dad was the Senior Sheep Shearing Instructor for

Scotland for a long time and, inevitably, I learned this skill too.

On one occasion, Dad appeared on Blue Peter as the reigning Champion Sheep Shearer and, after doing his thing for the activity slot, he met John Noakes, a very well-known and popular Blue Peter presenter. When he got home, Dad had a present for me. 'I asked John for a badge for you,' Dad said, 'but they told me they didn't have any spares.' Before I could get disappointed, he added, 'So I took his one off his blazer! Here it is!' I was amazed at my father's cheekiness. However, Blue Peter badges were worth far more than their weight in gold, and having John Noakes' presenter badge did lend me a certain cache.

With all these manly pursuits on the go, it was perhaps not surprising that Mum and Dad wanted another boy. The story goes that, when the nurse announced that they had a little girl, my mother asked her to check again! However, this was not entirely to my disadvantage. While I was greatly loved, my parents took a firm decision that I was not to be spoiled or wrapped in cotton wool, and they taught me all of the practical skills and independence that they would have passed on to their son. It was my dad who got me into welding and, without him, I might never have even considered working with aircraft.

However, when I told my parents I was going to the mission field as an engineer, they were less than thrilled. Dad blew his top and said some regrettable things; he would disinherit me and I would end up in the gutter. I told him I had never asked him for anything and that I wouldn't start now as God would continue to look after me and that I would keep coming to visit. I assured Dad that when I came he should know that it was because I loved him. Like it or not!

Mum informed me that they didn't want anyone from the church coming round to try to persuade them that either my faith or my plan of action was right. Their refusal to listen meant they never really got the chance to understand what I was doing and why I was doing it from my perspective, they only got it from my intermittent newsletters. It was over a decade before Dad spoke nicely to me again. I complained to God. 'It's me who needs the support. I'm the one who is giving up everything to do something challenging.'

He replied, 'But you know why and your father doesn't; it's your job to love him.' How could I achieve that practically? It's a difficult thing to put your mind to wooing someone who has set their face against you – the sense of injustice could have been paralysing if I was not so aware of the way the Lord had wooed me when I was against Him. I came up with the simplest plan imaginable: I would tell Dad I loved him every time I spoke to him on the phone. At first, he would just grunt but, after a while, he would wait to hear it. Sadly, every time I visited he would pick arguments and say hurtful things. I asked Mum if the problem was with me but she said no, it was with him; so over the years I just tried to be as respectful and non-combative as possible. I knew I couldn't return his anger with anger. For one thing, it's impossible to hate someone when you are habitually praying for them and, for another, I came to understand that the root of Dad's bitterness lay not with me but with the death of my brother. He was still scarred, and it was a pain that only God, not I, could deal with.

CHAPTER 4

A LEARNING CURVE

I gave several months' notice at work and, for some reason, I had it in my mind that I wanted to move out of my house three weeks before my last day at work. I thought I might sell it privately to save money for my training but I didn't take much action. There were three houses for sale next door and just across the road from mine and they had been on the market for almost two years, and nobody had been to even look round. It was obviously not a good time to sell. Eight weeks before my leaving date I caved in and went to an estate agent who assured me that it was not possible to complete a sale in five weeks. However, the signpost went up, and the next day someone came to have a look at my neighbour's house, which she didn't like, and so she rang my doorbell on the off chance of seeing round my home immediately, without notice. I was in, and she liked my house, offering me the asking price!

'There is a small problem though,' she told me, 'we need to move in five weeks' time!' As she was a bank employee, with the resources to make special arrangements, she managed to push the deal through and I moved out three weeks before leaving work.

Closing the door for the last time, I felt relief. It had been four years of no heating and not having the resources to complete the work the house needed. I got £9,500 from the sale. 'Lord, I put £10,000 in; I lost money on that house,' I told Him.

'But if I had sent you on a DIY course to learn how to be practical you wouldn't have stuck it,' came the reply. It was true. Because the house was mine, and because of limited finances, I had felt confident enough to have a go at lots of jobs. I had been able to make a mess and work my way out of it without any pressure from another person and, as a result, I was much more practical than I had been before.

Pat arranged a surprise leaving party. It was a huge surprise and really kind. About this time, three people came to me independently to tell me that God had a plan for me to get married. That was in 1992 and so, over the years, I reminded myself that Abraham had been promised a son with his wife but it took over 20 years before he saw the faithfulness of God fulfilled. God does not do things to our timescale or our plans, but He always does what He promises. I have learned the importance of listening very carefully to what He is saying and, once I am sure of a promise, trusting in it with all my heart.

Although my course was now set, it would take three years of training and waiting before I got a posting. Having confessed all of my past on the lengthy written application to MAF (and I needed the length), I went to All Nations Christian College. It was deemed necessary for me to attend a pastoral college to make sure that I wouldn't fall apart on the field.

For ministry practice I was placed in a traditional Anglican church. For someone from a very charismatic Assemblies of God style church, this could have been a difficult posting. However, the vicar, his wife and the church members were so wonderful and I came to the conclusion that anyone who can only worship God 'in spirit and in truth' in a certain style of service is always going to be vulnerable and could easily lose their faith. I embraced the differences and it was another stage in becoming a non-denominational Christian.

Many of my fellow students complained of the heavy workload. To me it all seemed a bit of a doddle compared with the life I had just moved from with a hugely busy job, dogs, church commitments, and experimental DIY. I deliberately limited the time I spent doing written work, preferring to focus more on the specific things I felt God wanted me to learn each term.

God's learning agenda for me was quite different from the formal courses. I did learn some really useful stuff in the classes. However, one term God said that I would learn courage, and I had a double-whammy crisis consisting of an operation to remove a lump from my leg, followed by a proposal of marriage which had to be turned down diplomatically. Not one of my better developed skills at that time!

I had a big question in my mind one day when I was sitting under a tree in the tranquil ANCC grounds and, as I pondered it, I couldn't understand why God had been silent on the topic and so I asked Him. 'Why won't you answer me, Lord?'

'What was the last thing I said to you?'

I cast my mind back and realised that months earlier He had spoken, but I hadn't liked the answer, so had ignored it. One of the first things a Christian learns about prayer is that God answers prayer in three ways – Yes, No, or Wait – but there is no pithy summary of the different ways we have of listening to Him. I found that sitting with unwanted answers takes self-discipline.

We had all sorts of practical classes: Dentistry, Midwifery, Car Maintenance, Hairdressing, etc. Whenever I wanted my hair cut I always had a great sense of urgency and, usually, my roommate Liz obliged. One day, however, she wasn't around, so I announced to a room full of assorted students that I would like a haircut and asked if anyone could oblige. One lady offered. She was nervous and to reassure her I said, 'Don't worry, you can't make a mess of my hair and, even if you do, I won't mind.'

Half an hour later I was crying in front of my mirror. My hair grows very slowly. I had spent two years carefully growing it so I could tie it back, and this dear lady had extended my fringe almost all the way round, like a monk's tonsure, so that I was faced with another two years' growth to restore any style. Then the Lord reminded me of what I had said. I had used words carelessly and had basically spoken untruths. I made up my mind to be more careful with what I allowed to come out of my mouth. Say what you mean and mean what you say!

After ANCC it was off to the USA. As a typical Brit, I held the view that the USA was the fount of all folly and things bizarre and I had always said it was the last place I would want to go. However, it was the first place God sent me from the UK and I fell in love with it.

I was there to attend a flight school approved by MAF UK. Most of the student pilots were European and were generally the spoiled and often wild-living children of wealthy parents. Most of the student mechanics were immature teenaged American boys, so living on campus was interesting. Thankfully there were a few more mature students, including Harry, a MAF pilot and Tim, another trainee MAF mechanic. I was the only female student mechanic in the school that year. Some of the men had a problem with that, especially when I got better grades than them. One called me 'Tool Waitress' and said that I was only awarded good grades because of being a woman. I told him not to massage his male ego at my expense!

The 13-month course was tough and intensive. If you got one test result below 70%, and couldn't improve it with a single re-sit, you were out. And it was very clear that 70% wasn't actually good enough, because that meant you were 30% wrong – not acceptable when maintaining aircraft. One minute late to class and you did an extra hour on Saturday morning. This rule applied even if you were ill or a close relative had died. The value of that was that one learned to work to the highest standard at all times and to shut out any possible distractions. I survived studying with 'flu and a painful condition that would have otherwise driven me to bed. It was a lesson that would serve me well through the many urgent needs and demands of life in Africa.

On my first Sunday in my new setting I thought I had better find a church, so I prayed and set off on my bike. In South Carolina most churches were still segregated, in practice if not legally, and, given a choice, I would have bucked the trend and belonged to a black church. However, on my way down the road I met a lovely dog and, as it started following me and wouldn't leave me, I went into the first church I came across where, having led me to church, the dog went home!

A mile from the college campus on reclaimed swampland, Oakey Swamp Baptist Church was mainly attended by two extended families. The pastor's wife intercepted me at the door and made sure that I knew whom all of the men were married to and stressing that they WERE all married! The only other single people were under 16, so I was incorporated into the 'young' married women's Sunday School class (in evangelical churches in America, Sunday School is for all ages) with ladies in their 40's and 50's. The hymns were all slightly country-and-western style. And there was a lot of eating. But they were openhearted and generous.

It was at this time that I fell head over heels in love with one of my classmates, Sammy. Ten years older than me, he was a kind, gentle and funny man of Greek parentage. We were attracted to each other the first time we met in class, but neither of us said anything. One day he asked me out to visit some local attractions, as I didn't have a car and went everywhere by bicycle. We started early and enjoyed a day of varied activity. We stopped on the roadside to smell some wild gardenias. We went to a large old house with amazing grounds and admired the massive alligators basking in the sun. We had lovely food in a restaurant that served, as a starter, boiled peanuts in their shells. Once the peanuts were eaten the shells were thrown on the floor and crunched under our feet. We saw a movie. We couldn't bear to part and so stayed out very, very late, always finding something else to do to prolong our time together. Eventually I couldn't stay silent anymore and blurted out my feelings as we walked along Myrtle Beach; and it turned out he felt just the same. There was just one issue between us – my calling to be a missionary, which Sammy did not share.

The encouragements I had had only three years earlier, of several people assuring me of God's plan that I would be married, kept occurring to me. This was a wholesome relationship, a true meeting of hearts and minds. However, I was here because of the certain knowledge that God had called me to a specific purpose, and I could not be derailed by the very sweetest of all inducements. What might have been right at any other time was not right for me at that point, and dear Sammy was too thoughtful and gentlemanly to ask me to give up the mission field.

Such bittersweetness was excruciating; all these years later, I can still taste it. Being so much in love, in class together every day, and yet not being free to be together forever. But in the midst of this big turmoil, God reminded me of the benefits He showers on His servants in even the smallest details of life.

After class I would often go out cycling on the paved roads around the college. There were no other cyclists, so I wore bright leggings to increase my visibility. One day I was talking to God as I was cycling. I was thinking that it would be nice to have some new leggings, and my favourites were to be found in a shop called 'Loud' in Cambridge close to my dear old friend Hils. I toyed with sending her a cheque and asking her to buy me a couple of pairs and send them out. Then I considered my limited resources and decided the idea was a bad use of short finances.

The next day one of my classmates told me, 'There's a parcel in the pigeonhole that might have your name on it,' and, sure enough, it did. The sender was Hils and on the green custom label it said the contents were leggings and t-shirts. They were from 'Loud' and I knew this was not a coincidence but a God-incidence that let me know how much He cared for me, even in seemingly trivial matters. He knew what would be on my mind and had prepared the answer even before I had got to the point of asking.

I had come to the USA with funds I had saved from the sale of my house. Partway through the course I ran out and it wasn't possible, or wise, to get an overdraft in the USA. I hadn't really prayed about what I should do and my room-mate ML, seeing my plight, lent me $50 to get food and I started to pray. I contacted my sending church asking for help in getting a loan, but they responded immediately by offering to pay my ongoing college fees and rent. That same week I was offered a cleaning job at the College that paid just enough to buy basic food and, in addition, my mother called out of the blue and offered to pay for flying lessons. I paid ML back and normal life resumed, albeit on a tight budget. When I stood up at church to give thanks for the kindness of God through others, they also surprised me with a collection and gave me over $800.

It was amazing provision but from then on life was harder work. College was 8am to 5pm. The cleaning job started at 5pm and finished at 8pm. I cleaned the Mechanics School, the hangar and, sometimes, the main offices to cover for an absence. Possibly because of cleaning the loos, I got a mouth infection. The doctor prescribed expensive medication. This being the US, I had a choice; buy the medication or food for the week. On the basis that I probably wouldn't be able to eat with the infection, I bought the medication. It worked well but I had little food. Then someone from Oakey Swamp came around out of the blue with several bags of shopping; they had been at the shop and just felt that they should buy groceries for me. They had no idea I had little money. My cupboard was full, and my heart was full of thanks to them and to God who had guided them.

Once, while I was house-sitting for friends from church, ML called in the middle of the night. 'Our home is on fire,' she said! I don't remember how I got there, but I arrived to see the firemen trying to control the massive flames shooting out of the roof of our flat and the dark night sky bright with flames. The painting that a friend, Liz, had painted for me years before (and which I had kept with me ever since) was the one thing that I was sad to lose. ML, on the other hand, was distraught about her weekly expanding collection of clothes.

When the flames were out we climbed up the charred stairs to pick our way through the deep charcoal and ashes on the floor of our flat. My borrowed bike, chained to the stairs, was trashed but the firemen had been thoughtful. Before turning on the hoses they had put as much as they could in the large cupboards in our bedrooms. My books and study materials and other possessions were unharmed, and even though the electrical switches had melted down the walls, Liz's picture was unharmed right beside them on the wall. Despite having most of her possessions intact, ML continued to fret. It brought home to me the importance of holding one's possessions lightly. The loss of mere material possessions should not be allowed to throw one into a spin and this is a lesson that has stayed with me ever since.

Power-plant lecturer Dave was an interesting man, a practising Catholic who commuted two hours to college and two hours back every day. This meant that he couldn't be much involved in his local church and he felt isolated; and the animosity between Protestant and Catholic isolated him even further as the vast majority of the staff and students, whilst not evangelical, still had a basic adherence to Protestantism. It took me a while to grasp that, just because they used a vocabulary that in a British person would indicate being born again, this wasn't necessarily the case in the US. Much of the time it was just words. Their actions betrayed a different worldview. However, I found speaking to Dave intriguing as his initial response to any question of theology that was posed in our little group of committed Christians would seem to be the opposite of ours. However, when we teased out the issues involved, we actually agreed on most things.

For example, one thing that came up was the doctrine of

perseverance of the saints; whether a person is 'once saved, always saved'. I would have taken this for granted, assuming that, 'Nothing can separate us from the love of God,' but Dave took the opposite position, believing it is possible for any Christian to reject God before death. There is more to the debate, of course, but it taught me not to be quick to judge others as well as confirming what I suspected from a childhood of separate schooling and disapproval of mixed marriages, that this sectarianism was a man-made barrier that I couldn't subscribe to.

In the meantime, I was learning God's answer to the Sammy affair. I made myself accountable to my friend Harry and his wife Willi over my relationship with Sammy. One day, towards the end of our time in the USA, Willi and I were talking it over. Willi felt God wanted me to 'lay it on the altar', just as He had asked Abraham to do with his son Isaac. However, when hearing from God on really important issues, I like to hear from a source which has no knowledge of my dilemma. I left her house pondering over what she had said, but aware that she could just be giving me her own advice. It wasn't what I wanted to hear, and I can be a tad slow in truly taking hold of what I don't want to hear.

Ten minutes later I was back at the home of one of our lecturers, Geoff, who was away on holiday and wanted someone to watch his house. I turned on the TV to find a programme on the life of Abraham was being broadcast, and I tuned in just as God was asking Abraham to sacrifice Isaac. Another God-incidence and, for the remaining months in the USA, I grappled with this. I kept hoping for a ram in the thicket, like the one provided by God that prevented Abraham from having to kill Isaac; but none came for Sammy and me.

At the end of our course Sammy and I drove through the spectacular countryside of several states to Maine so Sammy could eat a lobster, and then we drove back to South Carolina. It was a spectacular trip and we stopped in Washington DC to visit the Smithsonian (the Museum of Air and Flight, naturally). It was a long goodbye and leaving Sammy was excruciating.

I went back to Nottingham where I held a series of temping jobs, but I was just taking up time until my deployment with MAF started. My church graciously provided many things for me, meaning I was well-equipped for my journey, even down to a microwave oven (this was considered more a luxury than a right in 1995!). Indeed, I had a hard time narrowing down which things, on MAF's 7-page list of suggested items, were really necessary to take with me. However, on the basis that I was going to a poor country where I could easily give away any surplus items, I eventually decided to take a liberal amount of baggage.

The whole venture was filled with mystery, including how I would ever get really comfortable with my engineering work. I did not enjoy the prospect of feeling continually out of my depth while I honed my craft! I also read up on practical living skills, such as filtering all tap water to remove bacteria and soaking all produce intended to be eaten raw in disinfectant to kill off any nasties. I was acutely aware that any illness would waste not only my time but MAF's time, and I was equally aware that avoiding illness in the UK was a lot easier than avoiding illness in East Africa. Eight months was a long time to wait after finishing my training and yet it was hard to believe that the goal was finally in sight. On 5th September 1995, Hils drove me to the airport and off I went to Tanzania.

CHAPTER 5

MAF TANZANIA
– TO THE ENDS OF THE EARTH

I spent my first night in Dar es Salaam in another missionary's home, complete with internal lockable metal doors to impede thieves and sleeping under mosquito nets. Encountering these nets for the first time was a novelty which raised the question, do you tuck in the net first and squeeze under the last untucked edge, or sit in the middle of the bed and then tuck the net in under the mattress? One of many missionary controversies which no theological course covers!

Dar is the largest city in Tanzania, with a certain amount of Western luxury, beautiful hotels, and diverse shopping opportunities, including a department store. Dodoma, which was to be my centre of operations, is the formal seat of government, but is comparatively small and underdeveloped.

The morning after my arrival in Dar, we set off in the bright sun and tropical heat. It had been months since the last rains and, consequently, eastern Tanzania was a dry and dusty place with little greenery – except for the glorious flame trees. I marvelled at the sights and smells: the mud huts and workshops crowding the roadsides, the heaps of rubbish, the minibuses and lorries with interesting logos (my favourite can be roughly translated 'New jungle, same old monkeys', which can apply to so many of life's circumstances) jostling for road space, police road blocks where even the smallest transgression was seen as an opportunity for a bribe, overloaded bicycles swerving into our path and sizeable potholes that even a 4x4 needed to swerve around.

In stark contrast to all this chaos was an oasis halfway through the journey: a German bakery in Morogoro. It had pristine loos, cheeses and cured meats in chilled glass display cabinets, and an array of tempting Western-style gateaux that I found disappointingly bland.

Various curious rock formations, a sisal plantation and two sizeable trees are notable sights on the road to Dodoma, but the one most welcome to the weary traveller is that of Lion Rock appearing on the horizon. It is so named because, when viewed from this approach, it resembles the silhouette of a crouching lion. For all my years in Tanzania it never lost its association with being almost home at the end of a journey.

I was to live on a compound, and this had advantages in that services, security, help and advice were always available. My fellow MAFers had even stocked the house with essentials to get me started.

Hangar staff, being generally technical, had over the years adopted various extra roles. In MAF Tanzania, one of them was maintaining the 'Jesus Film' Equipment and a set of puppets. The ageing and much used generator, sound and projection equipment needed constant attention. Village pastors would come to the hangar to make bookings. As this was before the mobile phone era, there would be no further contact, so it was important that arrangements were made carefully and honoured punctually.

A week's holiday to find your way around and to settle in is compulsory. That weekend, I volunteered to go to a village with Jackson, one of the non-technical hangar staff. I had no idea what I was signing up to, but was eager to find out. I marvelled at the roads – both their near-impassable condition and their obscurity. 'Turn left at that thorn tree' was a typical instruction. The size of the ruts and potholes were amazing to behold, and occasionally one remembered the end of *The Italian Job*, with the van teetering halfway over a cliff – while it never quite got to that point, there were many close calls over the years!

The roads were poorly maintained and some, which were formerly surfaced using foreign aid, had disintegrated so that only a few feet of tarmac still remained, and even these were potholed. Dust builds up during the dry season, making it very similar to driving in snow, and the clouds of dust thrown up by vehicles are as impenetrable as thick fog so that anyone standing nearby must feel themselves to be in a minor sand storm. Then there were the other road users – cattle, goats, various fowl, meandering cyclists and dawdling pedestrians, none of whom were eager to move out of the path of oncoming vehicles. This has two possible outcomes; the driver hits the brakes and stops with great regularity, or someone or something dies! However, don't be misled by all the negatives. Assuming that one has a well-maintained vehicle kitted out with tools, etc., and that one is sensible, travelling was great fun. I would, given a choice of a nice tarmacked road in Europe and a Tanzanian bush road, choose the bush road.

After our adventures along the way we eventually arrived in the village with its pleasant smell of smoke, roasting goat, dried cow dung, and warm African bodies. Above us were pristine starry skies, the Milky Way clear with no electric light for miles. The darkness was profound; it seemed to move, the bush coming alive, as the natives emerged seemingly from nowhere. They simply appeared, in their vivid plaid tunics and shawls. They were coming to hear about Jesus.

This was the start of village ministry for me. It would become my particular love, then my calling.

My worldly goods arrived some five weeks after me with few breakages and losses. It was a most peculiar experience to rediscover things packed over three years ago. Having familiar objects made it much easier to feel at home; and it was an enormous relief to be reunited with my favourite old leggings – I was me again!

Working in the hangar proved to be very enjoyable because my colleagues were wonderful. Everyone had to be prepared to have their work checked because safety was of paramount importance, and two sets of eyes were better than one. This meant that one had to be humble enough to be corrected if necessary but, because it was the same for everyone, nobody could afford to be hard on anyone else. At first, I was pretty slow and had to ask endless questions, but my colleagues were encouraging and soon I was making progress.

Dodoma, being a few hours' drive inland, was dry but not too hot. The mornings and nights were cool and we often had breezes which helped. In fact, one did need a duvet to keep warm at night. In December Dodoma received its first rain in eight months. It poured and the thunder was right overhead. As I had been warned, my doorstep acquired a lake and visitors had to teeter along the edge of one of the plots before risking the shallows to get to the door. The rains brought out the scorpions, which were big and black. They weren't quick or aggressive, though, and could only cause major discomfort, not death.

Tanzanian life was a major change from my first trip to the African continent, visiting my father's Uncle John and Aunt Gladys in South Africa as a schoolgirl. They lived very much the expat lifestyle where there were formal drinks parties twice a day, 'Spots and Sundowners'. It was explained that I was expected to sip my drink to make it last and, almost every evening, we played pontoon using matches instead of money for bets. There were many visits to older people. One retired doctor's wife assumed that all children liked chocolate cake. I really didn't, but she had made it specially and insisted, despite my polite refusal, that I have a very large slice. Mum, who knew my aversion, didn't see fit to rescue me. I got it down retching, with the aid of several cups of tea. Through all of the outlandish things I was called on to eat while serving in Africa (of which more later), few of them were as unpleasant an experience as that chocolate cake.

On the compound though, life and food were relatively easy. I became known for the Western-style cakes I baked and was somewhat in demand for wedding cakes. It was possible to get a lot of Western things, at a price (Heinz baked beans, HP sauce, Abbey Crunch biscuits; fruit and vegetables were found in the market, which is best described as resembling a shantytown and had many interesting aromas), so homesickness could be kept at bay. My little house was quite nice, if a bit 'studenty', and had the very great advantages of microwave, freezer, washing machine, constant water and power supplies. Not everyone had these; some people didn't have water in their taps for many months. Many people didn't even have taps!

In my first three months in Dodoma I learned enough Swahili to hold a basic conversation with a shopkeeper, for example, and I made three visits to rural villages (I especially remember the disappointment of Jackson when we were returning late at night and I refused to run over a dik-dik which was in the middle of the bumpy track – they are a small, deer-like, apparently delicious tasting animal). I held the triple office of bridesmaid, chauffeuse and photographer at a 9-hour Tanzanian wedding where the bride and groom were expected to look mournful throughout.

For a Westerner, the sights of Africa are very strange. But it doesn't take long before the Maasai women, in their colourful wraps and veils called kangas, and mud houses become normal. The lack of material possessions here can be shocking, but in my opinion we pay a high price in the West for our comforts. I watched, with interest, the reactions of several Tanzanian friends to my descriptions of our society with all the pressures on youth, the corrupt media, legalised abortions...they were shocked!

African life soon became familiar without losing its charm and, when writing home after nine months, I realised that Dodoma felt like home.

CHAPTER 6

A NEW NORMAL

About 20 minutes' walk from the compound, along the disintegrating tarmac road and then a path and some stepping stones over a smelly ditch, was KLM, or Kanisa la Mungu. This was part of a large Tanzanian denomination established by the Church of God denomination headquartered in the USA. When I first walked in, not at a service time but just exploring, the only one in was the bubbly Pastor Dismus, who encouraged me in irresistible terms to attend the church. This was not a natural fit as few people spoke English, but then it was a good way to immerse myself in Swahili. The congregation numbered around 60, including the children, and the only other white person was an American nurse-midwife called Auntie Caroline. A veteran of over two decades in East Africa, when I arrived she was just leaving for a year's furlough. I ended up being somewhat in charge of her projects in her absence. The Community Health Evangelism committee was an education, and I learned to adjust my expectations of timekeeping and efficiency.

At this time there was also a temporary lodger in her home. Rachel was a Bible translator from Alaska and a supernaturally gifted linguist, working for Wycliffe. I remember a conversation we had one evening when I popped over to touch base with her. She had finished her current translation, and when I asked what the Lord had next for her, she said it was as though there was a blank sheet ahead of her, which seemed very odd to me in the midst of a clear call to Tanzania. The following week there was a car accident on the Dar road and Rachel died. She was only in her early twenties but it seemed that she had completed all that she had been on earth to do.

When I arrived in Tanzania there were a few nationals employed temporarily in the hangar, stripping paint off a Cessna 206 in preparation for a re-spray as part of the intensive Check 3 carried out every three years on every aircraft in the fleet. One of them was Joyce Mangu, a young lady related to one of the Tanzanian mechanics. A few weeks after my arrival the work was over and I felt God asking me to give Joyce a job in my home. Many people employed nationals as house girls, but I really didn't want one, being fully capable of doing all of my own housework. However, I felt God impress on me the importance of the job for Joyce, so I took her on. Looking now at the lists of jobs I asked her to do, I can see I had overly high expectations because of my inexperience; but dear Joyce was a hard worker and we got on well.

Eventually Joyce moved on to train as a Lab Technician and secured a very good job in Dar. It became clear that to really help, it is better to give someone a meaningful job with a proper wage. So after Joyce I took on Mama Selina for a short while until she also found a job elsewhere; and then I shared Emmie Kitundu with my neighbours until I took her on full-time as my housekeeper. Emmie had not had a good education. She was under-confident and always trying to borrow money to support her husband's business. The complications that arose led me to decide against loans for my staff. The alternative was to pay good wages and teach proper budgeting, with the understanding that help could be requested and might be given, and not loaned, for any real emergency.

Emmie and I worked well together over nearly 12 years. Because of my increasing involvement in village ministry we had lots of village people visiting at lunchtimes. Emmie's responsibility was to provide lunch, usually for about 10, but once we had over 30 unannounced and everyone was fed!

As well as providing food, we would read a Bible verse and then encourage discussion of its meaning over lunch rather than waste time on small talk which meant we had a lot of interesting conversations. Very often I asked Emmie to do things she thought she couldn't do. In this way, she learned to have a go before saying, 'I can't!' Emmie increased in confidence to the extent that she took on the Head of Church of God of Tanzania in a theological discussion and won! She also did the catering for our ministry teams during the big village meetings I organised over the years, including a final Pastor Meeting for over 200 people.

Work in the hangar started as soon as the first pilot arrived to get going in the morning, usually at sunrise, starting their aircraft. Living right next door to the hangar, and therefore the runway, one listened carefully. Was the mag drop OK? Did the prop cycle? If the noise wasn't right, one got up and dressed post-haste and went over to fix whatever was wrong so that the pilot could get on with their vital life-saving work. Officially, work started at 7am, with a tea-break consisting of freshly made *mandazi* (a divine African doughnut) at 10am, lunch hour at 1pm (often with many visitors at the house) and then work until everything was finished, anywhere between 5 and 9pm. After work I often had church meetings, usually unscheduled.

The history of Christian aviation is full of avoidable and often fatal accidents caused by enthusiastic amateurs. Part of the reason for MAF's existence is to provide a safe, reliable and professional aviation facility for medical and other essential services in places where commercial and safety considerations may prohibit other operators. In some areas we are the only mode of transport for vital medical and delivery services, as well as getting evangelists to their mission fields. It was a huge privilege to be part of the vision and to work hard to achieve our goals.

MAF could bring interesting new experiences to the natives. While running a women's conference with Auntie Caroline, I arranged for the rural village women to tour the facilities at the MAF compound. I showed them the hangar and ran a short class explaining how flight works and showing them the various instruments and parts of the plane, letting each woman sit in the cockpit. They were afraid! At the end of the demonstration one of our planes was going out, and so I'd arranged for the women to watch. They all stood at the end of the hangar, open-mouthed!

Another time one of the pilots was showing my pastor, Dismus, the inside of one of our planes, and, without telling him the plan, the pilot set off on a short flight. Dismus had never been in the plane before, but he took to it right away, landing in a state of euphoria. Years later he would travel to London with Caroline, a seasoned flyer.

In the time I served with MAF there was only one accident. I was the acting Chief Engineer that day and was called to the Radio Room just after 9am to be told a plane had crashed. The bottom fell out of my world, as she had just gone out after a check. All pre-planned procedures had to be gone through. It turned out that bad weather in a mountainous area was the cause and nobody was killed. But that much welcomed information came later after the stomach-dropping dread of bad news. Thankfully, because of our good radio coverage, emergency help got to the site relatively quickly.

I filled the role of Hangar Foreman for several years. It was a busy job, which had been somewhat neglected over a few years. It consisted of making sure that every mechanic's work was carried out to the best standards and to time, that double checks were carried out properly, that all of the required paperwork reached the office, that all equipment was calibrated annually, that all chemicals were labelled regarding their flammability and toxicity, that toolboxes were arranged so that missing tools would be easy to spot, that all spares were stored and labelled and processed correctly, and so much more.

We worked hard and diligently and earned a good reputation with the Tanzania Civil Aviation Authority (TCAA) as the best Approved Maintenance Organisation in Tanzania. When I first started, rather than making sure everything was done exceptionally well, people used to pray for favour with the TCAA – this was never the right solution and indeed was counterproductive. There are practical, as well as theological, reasons why we should do all things to the best of our ability, as unto the Lord. Our excellence in this area was a boon to our own infrastructure and a witness to the Aviation Authority officers, and it also illustrates why Christian organisations should always meet and exceed the standards of those around them.

It was a great relief when MAF decided, several years after my arrival, that everyone should have and maintain their own vehicles rather than relying on a shared pool of cars, and MAF offered to loan money for people to purchase from the old stock of MAF cars or get their own. I told God that I would rather walk or cycle than borrow money, and would wait to see what He would provide. As MAF budgets for overseas staff were generous I had, over the years, returned a fair slice of each month's allowance into my HQ account. I was pleasantly surprised to find out that what had accumulated covered the purchase of Matilda, a 12-year-old Land Rover that had recently been overhauled very well by my colleague Tim. She had no frills (including power steering or turbocharger), but was reliable over all of the years and many miles of off-road driving I did. Gradually she was kitted out with all of the items needed for every eventuality, including a specially designed film screen on the roof rack and film projection equipment.

One of the most interesting elements of Tanzanian life was receiving presents, which usually took the form of live chickens. In my first couple of years at MAF I received five, plus a cockerel and a guinea fowl! It was expected that one should cut the feathered offering's throat and enjoy a meal, but I could not entertain such an idea and so my garden was infested with chickens. The first had to be destroyed after next door's dog got it – an event which involved impeccable intersection of chicken flying over fence and dog simultaneously escaping from garden. The MAF guards enjoyed a meal! Three were donated by a family leaving the TZ programme, and remained in residence for some time. Another departing family passed me a further chicken; however, it seemed that she took exception to being henpecked and made a midnight getaway. Then arrived the cockerel and guinea fowl, both equipped with loud voices and escape tendencies. The latter, at least, was curbed by the use of my hairdressing scissors on his wings. 'Mr H' had a short but lively skirmish with the leader of his new and reluctant harem but eventually settled in, and the little guinea fowl was his favourite. Egg-laying was temporarily suspended due to the hostilities, and Mr H ate the three eggs which were being brooded by the hens prior to his arrival. He was an early and vociferous riser and was therefore confined to the bathroom at night to spare my neighbours. The hens, meanwhile, forsook their coop and took to roosting in the flowerpots and laying their eggs there to the detriment of the plants, which formerly had sole occupancy. Presents in Tanzania had wonderful comedic potential!

CHAPTER 7

THE COLOUR OF MONEY

A new Westerner in town was always an attractive prospect to professional beggars, who seek to make use of the period of ignorance until the person 'gets wise or cynical'. My first real exposure to this was a blind man who tried to con me out of hundreds of dollars. He was relying on the fact that new people often didn't have a grasp on the real cost of living for nationals, as newcomers tend to shop in expensive places. He said thieves had taken all his food. In fact, for my first eight months in Dodoma, nobody came to visit without wanting something – not even the Westerners.

One of the hardest things to get used to in Dodoma life was the number of visitors who arrived, unexpected and uninvited, although generally not unwelcome, at my door wanting me to give or do something (about four per day in the beginning). It made it so difficult to plan one's activities and it was not unusual for someone to turn up at a tea break, another one or two at lunchtime, and two or three after work. I had lots of people coming to my door asking for sponsorship for all sorts of things such as schooling, starting businesses, etc. It was very difficult to refuse without discouraging people from continuing to try to improve their lives in a constructive way.

As time went on I had a nearly inexhaustible supply of pastors coming to my door asking for funds for their projects or their livelihood, and often I would make a donation saying, 'I'm going to give this to you, but you have to tithe a part of it.' In this way, they learned godly stewardship and budgeting. If they came back asking for more money, I would want to know what they'd done with the first lot. One pastor came back saying, 'Matika, it works, it works! I tithed some of the money, and the Lord took care of me!'

It would be so easy to become cynical about the sincerity of friendships but, in my attempt to prevent this, I came to the awful realisation that I more often than not treat God in just the same way. How often do we spend time with God just because we want to be with Him and not asking for anything?

In a year with poor rains, the number of people begging in town rose dramatically and we had reports of people in nearby villages who were only able to eat once every three days. The famine in Tanzania was not on the scale of those that were widely publicised on television in the West, but it was just as awful for those individuals who watched their beloved relatives starve to death. Animal attacks also went up in years of drought, as lions and other beasts would kill humans for food. I started to wean myself off imported western goods and got used to cheaper local fare, as so many people needed help. A local committee was set up to import food into the region to help those who were in difficulty, as it was recognised that the government would be unable, or unwilling, to provide effectively. But it was hard to see famine close up, unable to switch off the TV when it became too distressing. Personally, I think it is a disgrace if one person should die of hunger in a world where there is more than enough to go around, and I hoped to help the villagers find ways to live less near the edge so that one year's bad rains would not mean disaster. However, as one of my colleagues remarked, it isn't easy to change habits of 2,000 years.

The number of attempted break-ins had peaks and troughs. When things got too bad, the Chief of Police would give an order that all thieves were to be shot and, after a few fatalities, things would quiet down until the next spate. In addition to the compound guards, who were supposed to patrol the boundaries all night (but were often caught snoring in their huts), we all had air horns in our houses that could be set off to good effect. The rule was that, on hearing an air horn, at least one occupant of each house would come out to reinforce the team of thief catchers/repellers. One Christmas we had seven attempted break-ins. It didn't lend itself to sound sleeping and to this day I have tendency to shoot out of bed if I hear anything in the middle of the night.

Burglary seemed to particularly flourish during the rainy season. Thieves in Tanzania, once caught by Tanzanians, receive no mercy. They are very often beaten or stoned to death and, although I have never seen this happen, one of my neighbours did. She was in the market and noticed the crowd suddenly start to move in an odd fashion. As they started to beat the thief, whom it turned out had stolen a tub of margarine from her basket, she tried to intervene and was almost beaten herself. However, eventually she and a local pastor rescued the man and took him to the police station where she was asked, 'Why didn't you kill him first before bringing him here?'

On one occasion, I was woken at 3am by the telephone. It was Caroline. 'The house has been broken into,' she announced. 'Ghanghai, the night watchman, has been hurt and there are four suspicious looking guys at the gate. I think they are thieves. Can you come and rescue me? Probably wise to bring one of the MAF guards with you.'

When we arrived, we found that the staff at the neighbours' properties had simply ignored the robbery. Eight thieves had gone into the yard, cut Ghanghai's knee with a machete, and hit him on the head with a hammer. They wrapped his head in a coat and stood over him discussing how to kill him. Still conscious, and a very finely built chap, he said to God, 'Are you going to let these bad men kill me?' Suddenly he felt like

Samson must have felt when his strength returned, and he got up and escaped over the gate despite the invaders' efforts to stop him.

The four men, still at Caroline's gate, turned out to be good guys, including an off-duty policeman who had risked himself to rescue Ghanghai. I went to check out the situation at the house and put Ghanghai in the back of Matilda, as he was bleeding, and we set off for the police station. In Tanzania you cannot be treated for a suspicious injury at a hospital without a form from the police. We got the form easily and made it to the General Hospital, where the staff were asleep and showed little interest in treating Ghanghai. Caroline donned gloves and got him cleaned up herself before motivating the staff to sew his wound.

Many people coming to Tanzania asked MAF for help with missions. Some Dutch students arrived looking for a project to invest in. The group of pastors in the Mkutani/Membe area near Dodoma had been asking for corrugated iron roofs, so I suggested they stay in the villages, buy the bati (corrugated iron sheets) and roof the eight or so churches. This was a huge help to our village churches and didn't put the students off as they subsequently came back a few years running. However, they changed to building orphanages.

Supporting orphanages was, and I believe is, very fashionable to Westerners. The nationals that have good communication skills, and know how to behave around foreigners, usually succeed in getting significant funding. In my experience these donations are usually used, at least partly, to fund private concerns. The funders are blissfully unaware and unwilling to listen as long as some progress is made on buildings or services between their visits. Nationals were quick to pick up any changes in current types of projects that Westerners would easily agree to fund. There were many stories told amongst them which were not meant for Western ears, but my Swahili was good enough to read between the lines. Many people felt that any *mzungu* should just cough up anything they thought to ask for, and I took to describing myself as *Ngozi rangi ya hela,* 'skin the colour of money'.

CHAPTER 8

THE WO-WO-WO

When I got to Dodoma I picked up some vibes and comments from the wives of MAF staff. There had been a single female who was too friendly with the men, and so I made a decision to keep my distance. As a young woman I had got a lot of attention – sometimes wanted, sometimes not – on account of the frankly unusual size of my chest. In my adolescence in Wigtown, my nickname was BT – I'll leave you to work out what that stood for. So famous were my assets that someone even went to a fancy-dress party as me, wearing Abba-style blue eyeliner and two balloons stuffed down their top. So, in Tanzania I was glad to remain under the radar; but that was easier said than done.

One day a guard came to my door to tell me about a chap who wanted to see me. 'I think you should come to the gate,' he said. It was clear he didn't think it wise to let the unknown visitor free access to the compound and my home. This fellow was dressed up to the nines and told me he wanted to get married – to me! It was common for Tanzanian nationals to see marriage to a *mzungu* as good luck and a meal-ticket to a wealthier life in the West. With this motivation they would often present themselves as potential suitors with a frankly unfathomable level of optimism. Now, I was well aware that most of these offers were made somewhat cynically, because it quickly became clear that I hadn't been designed to appeal to African ideals of beauty.

This may not be strictly within the bounds of political correctness, but it has become evident to me that many white people find it difficult at first to distinguish between black individuals, with their subtle differences in eye and skin colour and type of hair. It came as something of a shock to realise that they have the same difficulty with us. On my first day in the MAF hangar I introduced myself to the same hangar assistant three times before he put me right. My petite neighbour Jenneke and I were mistaken for each other, even though she has long curly blond hair and mine was darker, fine and short and I am of a bigger build.

Tanzanians also judge someone's age based mostly on their weight. They will often say, 'This is my younger sister but she looks older because she is so fat' – and this is meant as a compliment! If you come back from holiday they will say, 'You have got fat,' meaning you look good. As a *mzungu* one bristles at this compliment. We would prefer 'You've lost weight.'

I once went to the MAF store window to get an oil filter for the check I was doing. My colleague Mwankenja looked out at me and said, 'You look like a cat!'

'What nonsense. I look nothing like a cat!' I told him.

'It's your eyes. They are cold and *kali*!' This is a wonderful multipurpose Swahili word that can mean sharp/fierce/intelligent – or a plethora of other things depending on the context in which it is being used. 'It's their colour,' he added, meaning my eyes were blue rather than the usual brown.

This may at least have lent me an exotic air, but cats in general are not popular as they are seen as nosy, and often if they come exploring in someone's house, it is assumed that a malicious person has turned into a cat to spy.

On another occasion I had asked Mwankenja to get dust sheets to protect the upholstery of an aircraft we were upgrading. They were procured from the market and Mwankenja duly called me to inspect them. One was an attractive stripy piece of material. 'It's nice; you could wear it to go to town,' he said. So I wrapped it round my waist, African style, to please him. He scrutinised me very seriously indeed and then said, 'You don't look nice, you look like a schoolgirl; all dried up at the back!' Apparently, I didn't have the 'wo-wo-wo,' or attractive big bum.

Jackson Kadebe, another great friend and hangar assistant, used to pinch the skin on my arms and lick his lips extravagantly whilst saying the equivalent of 'Nyum nyum nyum. You have skin like a pig.' In fairness, this isn't far from the truth if you look at *mzungu* skin compared with darker skin. He also said my hair was like *katani*, the fuzzy cotton picked from Tanzanian fields before being processed into lovely cloth.

At one point, when I first joined the Sifuni Band (of which more later), we shared one miserable room in Chamwino and they borrowed my bike, camera and radio/tape deck. We were called to sing at a funeral not too far away; these were all-night affairs lasting until 6am. On our return to their room, it turned out that someone, knowing they were out all night, had broken in and stolen their and my stuff. My friend Richard and I sat talking outside for an hour or so, consoling one another. However, I was aware that he had something else on his mind as he was talking, and eventually it came out. 'I have never seen anyone with such a long nose as you!' Certainly, I admit it isn't the neat little button of many Bantu noses and so I realised that my plain looks were not considered attractive in Tanzania. A short summary of the above: 'I have been told that I have skin like a pig, eyes like a cat, hair like *katani* and that I have dried up at the back!'. This was useful as an icebreaker in later years when I ministered amongst people who had never had meaningful contact with a *mzungu*. The self-deprecation showed that I didn't take myself too seriously and was open to comments and even criticism – important when trying to build good relationships. With my job they saw me as an automatically elevated being, so to humble myself was to lift them up to equality.

I was occasionally appreciated for my finer qualities. On one occasion, I was giving talks in a bush village several hours outside of Dodoma. There were about 400 attending the seminars and it was the first time for many of them to have a chance to talk to a white person. We discussed lots of things, from training sheep dogs to courting, and had a most enlightening time. Several of the men went outside and began discussing me, and thankfully one of the ladies I was travelling with knew their tribal language, otherwise I'd never have discovered what they were saying. The conversation went something like this…

'Goodness me, our wives are uneducated fools! Have you seen her?'

'I can't understand why she isn't married.'

(We had discussed this at great length but they still didn't understand.)

'If I hadn't already been married I could've taken her.'

'But looking after a white woman…do you think it would be possible?'

'I have my doubts that she would be able to do the heavy work. She'd just sit around getting fat and after only two days (of marriage) it would be necessary to make her work by hitting her with a big stick!'

I nevertheless had a long series of offers over the years, which were a nuisance, but I dealt with them by being very frank and clear about my lack of intentions. I would then point out my unsuitability as a financial saviour and also the fact that I didn't even have time for people I wanted to spend time with, never mind making time for an unexpected suitor. I would then refer them back to God as the only true Saviour and the only one who could fulfil their desires. That would be enough to disabuse them of any romantic or financial notions.

The fact is that women in Tanzania have a very hard lot. Men tend to take it easy, and women do everything around the house

– it's not unknown for them to be out tending the garden hours after giving birth – but if you ask the man, he will say his wife does nothing! Wives have very few rights and are often beaten, and are also effectively silenced in public. When Caroline and I would lead community-based healthcare classes, we would ask the women to speak first and then the men, to make sure they had a voice. In marriage seminars we made them listen to each other, and the Christians did tend to do better. When Christ came into their lives, women found dignity.

At work my singleness was seen by the nationals as a sin. Being unmarried and childless was, it seemed, a contravention of God's command to Adam and Eve to go forth and multiply. My dear friend, Ruth McKelvey, the only other single woman on the compound during my first years there, suffered the same harassment. A primary school teacher, she took to answering the question, 'How many children do you have?' with '27!', or, in Swahili, 'Only God knows.' She was very hurt once at a conference when the nationals told her that, if a white man wouldn't take her, they'd find her a black man. It was a blessing that we had one another for mutual support.

We both got many lectures. In fact, I got them at every tea-time for months. I could not talk about the pain I was still enduring on leaving Sammy, but I felt the injustice of their judgement; my singleness was *because* I had obeyed God.

Tim, who had been on my course in the USA, joined our compound. One tea-time, when my lone estate was brought up yet again, this normally quiet man made a loud outburst which shut everybody up for good. While not in need of male protection, my protestations that the apostle Paul had advised Christian workers to remain single had fallen on deaf ears. I was grateful that the Quiet Man's uncharacteristic remarks had finally shamed everyone into silence on the subject.

When I turned 35 – the age when I felt it would be much harder to start a family – I faced up to the fact that, despite various offers of marriage, there had been none that I was prepared to give up any of my busy life to invest in. I do not regret not having children. My expressed lack of intention in that area had discouraged several suitors in the past. Had I married and started a family, I would not have been able to do the many things I was free to do in Africa, which I believe were God's will for me. I believe that family life and children are so important that they need proper investment and I wasn't prepared to do that and, instead, enjoyed the fruits of my freedom.

Looking back, I believe that the energy generated by singleness gave me the edge to achieve greater things at times. No doubt these experiences illustrate Paul's wisdom in his advice. Few young women these days consider the privileges and opportunities of Christian single life, and so become embittered when they don't see the Lord providing the companionship they so desire. I'm thankful that, my Sammy heartbreak notwithstanding, I had liberty in my spirit to do God's work unimpeded.

Certainly, there were many times when I struggled with loneliness or wondered when the Lord would keep His promise concerning marriage – I did not realise at that time just how much I was disbelieving the word I had had from Him in this respect – but they didn't distract me from my work.

I remember speaking to a single female friend about this in later years, and telling her, 'I have not sat around and waited for God to bring my life to fruition.'

'Yeah,' she replied wistfully, 'but I have.'

CHAPTER 9

FRIENDS: THE FAMILY YOU CHOOSE FOR YOURSELF

Auntie Caroline played a huge part in my life in Tanzania. She was a supersized personality; a single American nurse/ midwife/missionary, she had vast experience of African life. Her Swahili was more Kenyan and, therefore, considered basic for Tanzania (there is a common saying, *Swahili was born in Zanzibar, grew up in Tanzania, fell sick in Kenya, died in Uganda and was buried in Congo*), but she still managed to successfully counsel childless couples, and there were quite a number of little girls in our village churches called Caroline in her honour.

She often had interesting books open on her coffee table – including, memorably, a guide to sexual intercourse when heavily pregnant, complete with graphic illustrations. When we got together for Friday pizza evenings in her lovely home, they often involved her favourite birth videos. Because of her profession she was blissfully unaware of the comfort zone of nice middle-class Christians newly in from the West. She once said, in one such group, 'It's such a little hole, but it causes so many problems!' This is undeniably true, but jaws hit the floor. The room was speechless. This was a wonderful moment that I greatly enjoyed.

As mutual dog lovers, we brought two of her Jack Russell pups to Dodoma from Arusha by road – a journey of around ten hours. Frequent stops and lots of love got them there, and she was generous enough to let her dogs love me as much as I loved them. She kept a series of mutts too, always called Lady and Tramp. The last Lady wouldn't let anyone other than me touch her. One day I went to visit and she was under the hedge, tongue out, which indicated she was possibly poisoned or snake-bitten. I suggested the vet be called. When he arrived, he said he would put the dog down by injection if I caught her and put a muzzle on. I said I would if he could promise me she would die quickly. He promised, so I caught Lady, put the muzzle on, handed her over, and left in tears.

When I came back half an hour later, Lady was staggering round the garden and the usually stoic Caroline was sitting in a chair in the garden in shock, having been told that the vet would come back to complete the job tomorrow. I made a phone call to the vet, and having given up on him, then called our pastor, Dismus, to bring his gun. Lady was re-caught, placed in the grave the watchman had dug in preparation, and Dismus, himself looking sick as a dog, shot her.

Caroline and I went on holidays together. I would have roughed it in cheap guesthouses. The very cheapest was 60p for three of us on a trip to Mirambo, including secure parking for the Land Rover, mosquito nets, an electric light bulb, cup of tea in the morning, cockroach-infested long drop for a toilet, and the chance to wash with water from a concrete tank in the central courtyard in company with a Maasai warrior. For some reason, however, Caroline liked nice hotels at the beach in Dar, where she would turn the air conditioning to the coldest setting and I would take all of the available blankets in the room and get more from reception. It was good for me that she made me experience the nicer places.

Once we stayed in the Silver Sands hotel up the coast before it was renovated. The first day we were served tea with milk, orange juice, fruit, and bread with butter and jam. Each day there was less on offer until there was just black tea and dry bread. The trouble with hotels trying to be Western is that one can get food poisoning easily if they don't know how to keep leftover food safe. I got terrible poisoning from chicken and chips one evening. It was difficult knowing which end to put on the toilet, and it was all projectile, all night. Next morning I was faint and weak, but Caroline had glasses to pick up in town and wouldn't hear of me staying in bed, so I had to get up and go. It was tough, but Caroline had no sympathy, even with herself.

With her Community Health Evangelism, Caroline had a team of dentists over once a year. She kindly included me as driver, interpreter and general organiser in villages. We would pick up the team in Dar and head for Dodoma to prepare, and then out to villages. In some places, the patients were nervous as they had experienced extractions without anaesthetic; so we had to persuade one brave person to go first and tell the others it was okay.

In Membe, a KLM pastor called Samson came to the dentist. His naturally broad face was unnaturally flat, and he had open running sores in several places. His shirt collar was soaked in pus. It turned out that he had had just one bad tooth for several months and his father would not sell any of his livestock to pay for treatment, so he had sat in great pain waiting to die. The dentists said he needed to go to hospital, but nobody wanted to be in a vehicle with him in case he had TB, so I volunteered to take him to Dodoma, along with his cousin Kenneth, also a KLM pastor.

We drove through the night. I remember it well as the dentists asked Samson to wear a mask to protect us from infections, and we stopped to view a bush fire which crackled loudly and shone in the dark, generating a lot of heat. I had them stay in my wee place, sleeping in the living room, one on a camp bed and one on the sofa. I took Samson's clothes and washed them as they stank of rotting flesh. The next morning he was admitted to the Dodoma General Hospital. Mosquito nets, vacuum flask and other essential supplies had to be acquired and were generously paid for by the dentists.

We left him in the hospital's care and then set off on the next part of our dental trip. Many people who had suffered greatly were helped and we had a lot of great experiences, including giving a lift to a cattle-herding Barabaig family who had never been in a vehicle before. They were all dressed up in goatskin skirts and blankets, covered in rancid milk fat, and their heads shaved with just a ball of hair left at the back of the skull. The granny got carsick, and when I stopped Matilda to let her out, her grandson watched how the door was opened. When we finally got to their destination he was overjoyed to do it for himself. How fantastic to be so easily pleased!

On return to Dodoma I found out that Samson had got medication, his tooth extracted, and he had gone home well. I could hardly believe it. However, there was more to come. A few weeks later, I was having a very long, tough week at work and found out at 5pm that we had been given the wrong inspection paperwork for a Cessna 402, which meant working late so it could be signed off and flown the next day. Because I was tired, I had carelessly bent down and hit my head on a window frame. A trickle of blood ran down my face as I adjusted to the pain in my head. What a day!

Wending my weary way home (all of a one-minute walk), I saw a figure sitting on the seat outside the door of my wee house; a visitor who would inevitably need food and help. It was Samson, with a white thing on his lower jaw. We exchanged greetings, I offered him hospitality, and then he said, 'Sister, have you seen this?'

He angled his now very bony, uninfected face up to show part of his jawbone protruding through his skin. So it was back off to the hospital for an operation to remove part of the bone, sew the skin back and more medication. He also had a hernia that needed fixed – all at my expense. It isn't easy to be kind when you're tired, but the Lord gave me the grace! Thankfully, medical expenses are not huge in Tanzania, and he did get better. However, his teeth were always loose and at odd angles thereafter, so he ate with great care and trouble.

On another trip with dentists, Auntie Caroline got cellulitis and was in Seliani hospital in Arusha in severe pain. I stayed for a week to look after her, sleeping on cushions on the floor of her room. She complained not once. Another time, in Dodoma, her temperature was so high she was bright red and delirious, but she was as stoic as ever. I was not keen for her to die on the field and was glad when she went home permanently to the USA, toward the end of my time in Tanzania, at the request of mission team leaders concerned about her health. At that time the political situation in our area was shaky and mission organisations were considering sending their representatives home. I was relieved to know that Caroline, now in her 60's, was safe.

Early on I went to language school in Morogoro to learn Swahili. At school, I had never been good at languages and this was no exception. I came away after several weeks completely unable to speak Swahili. 'Lord, you called me here to be an evangelist and I can barely go down the market and buy carrots, never mind tell people about you! Help!'

As ever, the Lord had His own crash course ready for my enrolment. Every day at the hangar I would see a vivacious, attractive woman coming in to sell her delicious *mandazi* and *chappati* in our tea room. She was always smiling and chatting to everyone. 'Who is that woman?' I asked Henry Kambenga, one of our temporary hangar assistants. 'She looks so bright and happy – I'd like her to be my friend.'

Henry began to laugh. 'That's my wife, Ruth,' he said. 'I'll introduce you, but you must come to dinner and know her better!'

Ruth Kambenga quickly became my best friend in Tanzania. The Lord's plan for me to learn Swahili was to give me the chance to drive for the Sifuni Band, which Ruth and Henry managed.

Yohanna, Danny, Mwankenja and Richard were great musicians. Their Christian songs were highly popular wherever we went and attracted huge crowds. We went to villages many weekends to bless the villagers, no charge. Not understanding

Swahili at first, I used to just sit and observe. We went to every type of church denomination and it was good training for what came later in my career. We also went to overnight celebrations for weddings and funerals. There was a lot to learn about any new culture, and having nationals close enough and open enough to explain the subtleties was rare and invaluable. I learned about how to behave in African churches, about table manners and about village living from an African perspective.

The Sifuni Band gave me a name from the local tribe. *Matika* is the name given to a female child born at the time of a good harvest (which is rare in Dodoma, where two out of three years have poor rainfall and little if any harvest). In short, the name means Grace, as does Anne. I was often hailed *Matikagwe*: hey you, Matika! For years, all nationals called me Matika and all Westerners called me Annie.

For five years I was on the band's management team and provided basic finances for the four musicians and the evangelist who accompanied them. It was an enriching time of great friendship – with many complications. The evangelist betrayed the trust that had been placed in him when he impregnated a girl who had made a commitment at a meeting where he had preached, whilst his wife was expecting. And then, he sent the girl back to her family with no support offered. Not a good example of what a Christian should be! He was, of course, unable to continue with the village ministry and never showed any remorse. The Anglican Church in Dodoma, however, gave him a good position.

Ruth and I had decided early on that I would teach her English and she would teach me Swahili. After the evangelist, who was very loud and exciting, departed, I started preaching in English on the band's tour, and Ruth would translate for me. Although her English was basic, Tanzanians have a particular knack for communication; besides, sometimes God aids in translation! In any case, our theology was so compatible that, as long as Ruth knew more or less what I wanted to say, she could fill in the gaps herself. The first time we tried this, 16 people came to faith. The band members said, with characteristic finesse, 'It was the Lord's doing – it couldn't have been you, Matika!' This was not flattering, but it was true, and good to know the Lord was working through (and despite) our best efforts.

We tried this method twice, and on the third trip, Ruth said, 'You will preach in Swahili now. You may not be very good, but I'll write down anything you have a problem with and we can go over it later. I'll summarise at the end and make sure they understand everything important!' So, with fear and trembling, I preached for the first time in Swahili. I never stopped!

In the villages, nights were often disturbed because of being obliged to share cramped quarters with fleas, bed bugs, maggots, mosquitoes, cockroaches, earwigs, and not least, strangers. Once we stayed in a hut with 19 lively piglets that spent the whole night noisily rifling through the kitchen, eating off the plates we would use for breakfast. When we left, everything we owned smelled of pig. In remote areas the unwelcome sound of rain, which could render just-about-passable roads life-threateningly dangerous, would cause me to lie awake praying for safe passage.

Henry Kambenga was self-supporting, but because their engagements required being away for whole weeks in villages, the other chaps were unable to have full-time and permanent employment. They were all just starting out in life and had very few things at all, and indeed had been living on a distressingly low income. However, they had shown their commitment to the Lord's work, and the quality of their music was really good. I sent a list of things they needed and wanted – in that order – back to supporters in Scotland. Notable among the latter were sunglasses and bum bags, to look cool (it was 1996!). Besides the donations, they got a real boost from knowing people in the West were interested in their work and praying for them.

Ruth taught me some manners for eating Swahili food; for example, their thick, ubiquitous maize porridge, *ugani*. You have to form this into a ball and mix it with soup or vegetables. Without Ruth, I would have just spooned it into my mouth with my hand to the horror of everyone around me! However, I was able to return this favour. When we went to villages we were often given huge meals that Ruth, who had a dicky tummy, couldn't eat. To refuse what we were given would have been rude, so I would eat her leftovers. Because of this I likened her to a nibbling mouse, hence her nickname, *Panya Mdogo* (small mouse); the name stuck and many others used it.

For years Ruth and I fasted and prayed regularly for all of our work and felt that spiritually we resembled twins. I came to know her family, and her father said to me that I was now his daughter, a statement that cannot be taken lightly with the intimate family ties in Tanzania. I am thankful to have had a number of spiritual fathers, as that dimension wasn't part of my relationship with my own dad. When Ruth went to Babati to teach at my church's headquarters, the ladies who attended the seminar told me later about this lady from Dodoma who was just like me despite having black skin.

Ruth also often ministered to those who were sick, uneducated, and outcast from society. She told me one day she was going to see Monika, who had been in the church choir but had been too ill to attend for a few weeks. The report Ruth gave the next day was so bad that few would believe it without seeing, and certainly I didn't. Many such reports that we get in Tanzania are exaggerated or inaccurate and one learns to be cautious. However, the following weekend, I was teaching seminars at their church and during a break went to visit Monika.

We arrived at the ramshackle collection of low mud brick and rusty corrugated iron-roofed buildings and sat on the short three-legged stools provided in the tiny litter-strewn yard. It was a big surprise to find that Monika was an albino, but a bigger surprise still was that her cheek was a huge raw mass with a hole right into her mouth. I was initially sitting downwind but had to move, as the smell of rotting flesh was unbearable.

Enquiring after someone's health in Tanzania implies that one will help, so if you don't want to help you shouldn't ask questions but merely sympathise. This was so bad that questions were inevitable and we managed to find out that the local hospital had, just a few months earlier, referred her to a place in Dar, but the family had not sent her.

Her sister, who had undertaken to nurse Monika, had a house full of relatives, some with special needs. Monika's elder brother had a job but needed the income to look after his family and he was not popular with the family as he never gave even a little something for soap or medicines. Later, however, once we started helping with the medical expenses, he wanted Monika moved to his house so that he could get some of the money for himself. This may seem shocking but, in fact, was very common. A sick or needy relative can be used to bring income to a family. Even the lady serving at the local dispensary increased some prices so that she could take the excess for herself without the boss knowing.

A pastor from my church in the UK kindly sent some money, and Monika went to Dar, where she underwent radiotherapy, but the outcome was not good. Given the choice of having chemo or staying at home, she chose the latter! The main problem was getting enough morphine toward the end, which was only available from the hospital which she had attended in Dar. The nurses at the hospital had got hold of the initial prescription, and instead of getting the three bottles she should have been given free, they filled her existing bottle from someone else's on the ward, discharged her and kept the prescription for themselves, presumably to sell. Her sister Elizabeth was too ill-educated and powerless to do anything about it, and in any case her eldest daughter had just died of an HIV-related condition, so she was still dealing with the grief. Monika went to the hospital again once the bottle was finished, but managed to steer clear of the corrupt nurses and got three full bottles.

As it happened she only needed one before she died very

peacefully after a courageous, if short, life. A couple of days before she went she started saying, 'Jesus, God has sent you to take me – why are you walking so slowly?' She left one son, Jeremiah, whose father will never be known. Nobody in their right mind would own up to fathering the child of an albino. The stigma is just too great.

Friends from 'T Street' came out to visit and we spent a week in really poor villages about 100 km from Dodoma. We taught seminars, ran a children's programme, showed the Jesus Film, and the Sifuni Band played their music. We lived in the local pastors' houses, which were smoke-filled and insect-infested, and ate only the local food, including stew made from rotten goat meat.

Yet, we had a fantastic time and over 2,000 people responded to the Gospel over the week. The old men said they hadn't seen anything like it in their lifetime, and the pastors were inundated with people wanting to know when we would come back.

The MAF team could see that something special was happening with my part-time ministry and gave me a full month off to devote myself to it, at considerable sacrifice to the other staff. The Lord had called me to be an engineer, but He was slowly clearing the path and building up my experience for another ministry.

CHAPTER 10

HOME AWAY FROM HOME AWAY FROM HOME

The MAF Chad programme had only one aircraft mechanic. Eventually it had no mechanic at all, which meant that the planes would be grounded. MAF Tanzania had lots of mechanics, so those of us with American licences, and more than five years of practical experience in MAF, volunteered to take turns in Chad while MAF recruited a new full-time person.

My first trip to Chad was supposed to be for six weeks. It lasted for three months. Every month the Programme Manager would ask, 'Can you stay another month?' How could I not? If that was where the Lord needed me to be, who was I to turn Him down?

I mistakenly thought that, because I felt at home in Tanzania, I would find Chad the same. But Chadian culture was very different and far less easy-going. The country was permanently on the cusp of civil war. Every night the main roundabouts in the city were occupied by soldiers, armed and drunk or stoned, stationed to prevent rebels entering the city. They stopped every vehicle, sometimes making occupants get out as they searched for something. They wanted money and MAF staff did not pay bribes. The only solution was to approach slowly, stop exactly where they were so they didn't have to walk to you, switch the vehicle off, wind the window right down and extend a friendly hand with a relaxed smile.

MAF had an extensive manual about what to do if civil war erupted, e.g. leave vehicles unlocked but disconnect batteries if time permitted, where safe bases were (US Embassy, designated sites guarded by the French military from which evacuations might be arranged), and so on. As the hangar was seven kilometres from the MAF residential compound and offices, on several occasions when civil war seemed imminent, the Programme Manager called me to the office and told me to be sure I could survive at the hangar for three days with sufficient supplies of drinking water, food and bedding.

One of the pilots' wives told me that at that time N'djamena, the capital city where we lived, was one of the world's top ten worst places to live. I passed on this useful information to God, remarking that surely it wasn't a wise thing to be there. 'I know,' He said, 'but the safest place for you to be is always in the eye of My will.' I understood this did not mean immunity from injury or trouble, but instead that whatever happened, He would be able to keep me through it.

Apparently, when people had heard that a woman was coming to look after the MAF aircraft, they decided that was impossible and that MAF would, therefore, shut down operations. As a result, I became a tourist attraction, with many coming to check me out at the hangar. 'Can you really fix that?' they would ask. 'Why don't you stand and watch,' I'd reply. 'If you don't see me do it, you'll never believe it.' So they decided that a woman could fix aircraft, but as it was such an awful place to live, they needed to find an explanation as to why she would be doing it there. She must be an American spy and, as she refused all their offers of fathering her child, she must also be a lesbian. Eventually they decided, no, I was more like a nun. The staff, however, called me *Patronne*, French for 'boss'. The sense of authority was very important, and all the more so for a woman and a lone mechanic.

Daniel, my hangar assistant, lived in Walya with his lovely wife Suzanna and their five children. He was traumatised by his early village life. His elder brother was a rebel against the government under dictatorship. Daniel was often mistaken for this brother and his life was in danger from the authorities, who were hunting down his brother to kill him. He saw men shot out of trees like monkeys and people tortured. His parents sold all they had, including their supply of food, put the proceeds in his hands, and sent him off to the city to preserve his life. He made good by getting a job, marrying, building a home and having a family. He was funny and kind. He could be sent off on procurement trips around town and would patiently do whatever was necessary to get what we needed. This was no easy task in Chad.

However, in the hangar he was a liability. His mind was unable to grasp the basic concepts required to be a mechanic. I tried getting the Toy Boy (of whom more shortly) to give personal tuition, but even he admitted defeat. Daniel memorably once showed me how he checked the batteries used as backup for the MAF main office computers when the mains power went down. There was an ancient hydrometer with no sign of markings on it. He sucked up some battery acid, held up the glass to eye level, looked at it, said 'OK,' and put the acid back.

'How do you know it's OK?' I asked.

'I just do what the last mechanic did!'

Copying an action with no understanding of the underlying principle isn't good when the office computer system is involved, but imagine how much more serious when it involves aircraft operating in hostile environments.

I ordered a new hydrometer with the required markings on, checked the acid, and adjusted it to make sure our computers would be safe. Poor Daniel just couldn't understand the markings even when we drew them out on paper for easier viewing. Lovely man as he was, and much as I needed help, there was a huge pressure on me to make sure anything he did was checked well.

On the way from town to our compound, we had to drive

past the Presidential Palace inhabited by Deby, the erstwhile dictator. There was a stretch of road, with a sign at either end, announcing that it was a no-stop zone. Stop and you would be shot, no questions asked. One day when Daniel was driving, my attention was drawn to a light on the dash of the Toyota Hilux. The fuel gauge showed empty! *Daniel!* He just laughed, and thankfully we made it to the end of the no-stop zone and to a source of diesel.

Closer to the MAF compound there was a stretch of dual carriageway. In the blazing sun, on the pavement separating the two carriageways, sat a lady dressed in knotted plastic carrier bags. She also had a few bags containing whatever she had seen fit to pick up and carry with her, plus a metal pot for scooping water out of the sewers beside the road. There was a slick of fluid fanning out from where she was sitting. I was tempted to stop and offer assistance, but Daniel told me that she would just run into the stream of fast-moving traffic and perish. Apparently, she had been unfaithful to her husband, who had cursed her that she might die in the sun. And here she was fulfilling it alone, eating what others threw out, drinking raw sewage mixed at times with rainwater, and in the utmost poverty and discomfort. I have never felt justified in feeling sorry for myself since seeing her predicament.

I went to church at Walya Trois with Evariste, the MAF Staff Manager, and Daniel. The church there had a particularly militaristic feel. We ladies had uniforms to wear on Sundays with special offerings and/or communion. I found it difficult to know when to wear mine. Added to this, ladies were not allowed to speak in church or lead anything. Everyone was aware of the potential for any guest to be a spy for the Muslim dictatorship, so words were spoken with great care.

During the Harmattan season, winds picked up dust from the desert and blew into town. It was like a pea-souper or Scottish haar – you couldn't see far at all. Everything was coated in a not-so-fine layer of dust, even in the house behind closed doors and windows. Serial colds were prevalent. You just seemed to get rid of one and another was upon you. People said it was because the winds blew in bacteria with the dust.

At times the insect life proliferated. Any light shining into the dark night attracted swarms of buzzing, flitting, crawling bugs. The rays from streetlights seemed almost solid masses of insects. It was paradise for geckos, so at least someone was enjoying it. If there was a job in the hangar that required working after dark, it was truly unpleasant; hot, humid, the air swarming with insects and, alongside them, numerous toads all over the floor attracted by the concentration of food. I once moved a heavy stand and crushed several toads who, unbeknown to me, had installed themselves under it. There was carnage! A hammer had to be used for humane purposes. I felt wretched about it and, thereafter, exercised great caution.

One Fourth of July I went to an American Embassy 'bash' with my small group of friends; Italian Marcella, the wife of a banker, who had a macaque chained to a tree in her garden; French Canadian Armelle, the kind, outspoken, funny but insecure wife of an oil worker; and French Katja, who ran an estate agency in Chad. Armelle got me togged up in trendy clothes and off we went. It was a hot and humid evening. We shook hands with all of the dignitaries, who stood in a line along the path to the entrance of the garden. There were burgers and all manner of American food. The other missionaries were dressed in the usual bright baggy Chadian dresses.

The girls offered to introduce me to the French Ambassador. As I shook his hand and said 'Enchantee,' a beetle hit the back of my throat. I stood there with a fixed smile, considering the options; I could cough and spit and make a scene, or swallow the beetle. Decision swiftly made, I swallowed hard. The poor beetle, on its descent into my stomach, released a bitter chemical. Still polite, calm and smiling, I gratefully accepted a piece of chocolate cake that helped with the terrible taste. However, it was a wasted effort. After the Ambassador had moved on I told the girls about having to eat the beetle alive and, of course, they retold the tale to the man himself.

Emmanuel, an eloquent and charming 24-year-old officer in the Chadian air force, decided to make advances. To my way of thinking there was something strange about a man of his age chasing a woman of 40. However, I was told that it is common for Chadian men to lie about their age, much as many Western women used to do. And he did look much older. When he made his intentions clear I made my lack of intentions equally clear. It did no good. I nicknamed him 'The Toy Boy'.

One day a small soldier came to the MAF hangar. He asked for a lift into town, but he was armed and I refused to take him with the gun. He took the magazine out of the gun and gave it to me. Daniel sat behind him in the pickup while I drove, just in case he made trouble. Daniel was strong and very quick. When we got to town this man then wanted us to take him to our compound, but I refused and dropped him off in town as he had originally asked.

Afterwards Daniel and the hangar guard told me off. He had probably wanted to steal the car, or find out about the compound, so he could come back at night with soldiers to take whatever they wanted. Next time he came to the hangar dressed in a white robe. I greeted him respectfully, with a kind of African curtsey, thinking he had come unarmed. Daniel pointed out that he had his gun under the robe, so I frisked him, found the gun and insisted he leave the hangar. After that he came back without a gun, but I always frisked him to check, which he seemed to enjoy!

A member of the same tribe as the Chadian dictator, he gave me his phone number, saying that if anyone ever hassled me I should call him and he would deal with it. Thankfully I never needed it – and who knows what might have happened to the person who had crossed me! He also asked me to be his second wife, but I declined politely and christened him 'The Second-Hand Husband'.

All things considered, I had a real market in repelling potential African suitors.

Just before I left Chad for the first time I invited the soldiers who had been regular visitors to the hangar for soda and nibbles. The Second-Hand Husband came with his gorgeous little doe-eyed daughter.

Daniel said to me, '*Patronne*, do you know who that man is?'

'No.'

'The head of security for the whole airport!'

That was Daniel; enjoying the joke of me frisking this highly influential person.

I was taken aback, but then realised I got away with it because I had truly had the confidence that I was in charge and had the right to say what went on in the hangar over which I had stewardship. And the Second-Hand Husband had co-operated. Confidence and self-assurance, when based on solid ground, are great assets. With them one can achieve a great deal.

Another example of this was when a guy, armed like Rambo, came from the President's Palace with money to be transported in the badly maintained plane next door. As there were no staff in evidence there, Rambo sauntered into the MAF hangar and, standing right next to a fuel tank vent, lit up a cigarette. My only thought was to move him ASAP so I placed my hands on his chest and gently pushed him out of the hangar. I then squatted in submissive African woman style, looked him in the eye and pointed to the no smoking sign. Thankfully he understood and smiled, and I didn't get shot!

My time there ended with a trip into the air above Chad, both breath-taking and nerve-wracking. Several thousand feet beneath us the waterlogged countryside, with mud huts perched on small islands of dry land, gave way to a green wilderness with the occasional farm. These were hundreds of miles from the nearest neighbours, with no road and no contact with the outside world. How do people survive in such places?

I was also glad it wasn't my job to be a MAF pilot; all that freight to weigh and load in the heat, trying to be polite to passengers at all times, even when hassled, long hauls over terrain with no landmarks to make navigation easier, and at the end of the journey, unbelievably short grass strips. Not a job for the fainthearted! Mind you, engineering had its downside, e.g. learning to live with the dreadful responsibility of their lives in my hands. But, after several years on the job, I had grown in confidence and skill. Everything that was in my control was done to my best ability, and everything outside my control was in much better hands – for I firmly believed that God was the best engineer MAF had.

CHAPTER 11

ATTITUDE SICKNESS

For nine months I was seriously ill. The western doctors I saw relied on the blood tests from MacKay House in Dodoma, which suggested that I had malaria. None of the seven treatments they tried worked and they were panicking. I was wiped out by the medication. All I could do was lie in bed and then I heard startling words in my head from God: 'I am going to win this argument!'

What argument?

After some thinking, I hit upon one issue where I had not let Him in. After all of the hurt over Sammy, I had felt betrayed. It had taken four and a half years before I stopped feeling emotional pain over that parting and I had been criticised by those who didn't know what I was going through. When I had fasted and prayed for healing, all I had was a scripture saying that 'I would see the results of the suffering of my soul and be satisfied' – but no instant pain relief. Over those years it had taken all of my inner strength just to get up every morning and behave normally with people around me, and to build my new life in Africa. So, despite the promises from the years ago about getting married, I had shut off this possibility and would not let Him into that one part of my life. Then He said, 'I have killed people for less!'

This is true. The case of the cheats Ananias and Sapphira

in Acts, and Uzzah who was fried for touching the Ark of the Covenant, came instantly to mind, and I had a revelation of my own arrogance in arguing with the Creator. And then He let me know that I had been sent to bed much like a naughty child until my attitude improved.

I thought, 'I'm going to be in bed for quite a while, with that much attitude.'

One day, Ilonka, the Chief Engineer's wife, was tending to me. 'What happens if something serious happens?' she asked.

'You mean if I die?'

'Yes.'

'But I'm not dying! God hasn't told me that I am!'

'Matika, you have all the signs that you could die anytime.'

Unlike Rachel, I did not see a blank sheet in front of me. But, at this point, I knew I should leave Dodoma.

A normal Home Assignment is part of missionary life. After a hugely challenging and tiring time 'on the field', staff return to the countries where their supporters are based to promote the work, give reports and reconnect with donors. Just preparing for all their tasks to be covered in their absence is more hard work (most are involved in many good causes above and beyond their official job) and they arrive exhausted in their countries of origin, fulfil demanding schedules, and then return to resume their busy roles. One also has to spend as much time as possible with friends and family, probably several short visits rather than one long session, to hear what is actually happening and build up to meaningful conversations and maintain relationships. The first time I returned to the UK from Tanzania, three years after I left, I sent a list of answers to the most commonly asked 'Home Assignment/furlough questions' in my newsletter:

– No, I'm not brown at all as the sun here is strong and I'm avoiding skin cancer as much as possible. (One of my friends in Tanzania had bits cut out of him because of overexposure.) – Plus, I don't have time for sunbathing.

- No, I haven't met 'the right person' and am very happily single. But I'm pretty fed up with marriage proposals – 7 so far!
- Yes, I'd love to come for a meal, but I really don't need to put on any weight – in fact, I'd like to lose some. Most missionaries put on loads of weight because of the wonderful 'home' meals they get during furlough – help!
- No, I don't live in a mud hut. My house is very normal, made from concrete and has electricity, hot and cold running water, a deep freeze, microwave etc...we even have a swimming pool on the compound!

But that's all for a normal Home Assignment. This, by contrast, was urgent medical furlough. On arrival in the UK I was straightaway whisked off into solitary confinement in the London School of Tropical Health and Hygiene infectious diseases ward, where the Consultant was a friend from 'T Street' who brought me a stash of very welcome chocolate biscuits. All medication was stopped, I was poked and prodded, many blood tests were carried out, and a viral infection (virus now gone) was diagnosed. All the previous meds had only served to make me very ill indeed. My short-term memory was non-existent and I was hugely fatigued.

The Consultant was a wise man. He told me that he couldn't predict if or when I might get better, but suggested that people with a positive attitude usually did best, and then he left me to work it out on my own. This was achieved through more God-incidences.

I visited a friend in Andover who left me in a church cafe when he went off for a meeting and I got talking to one of the staff. She had come back from the mission field because of ME and, through talking to her, I realised that I was suffering from the same problem. She and her father, a minister, prayed for me. Then, a friend from Nottingham, having heard of my predicament, sent me a book written by her friend about ME which had lots of helpful advice that truly, albeit slowly, helped me improve.

On release from hospital I went to stay with my parents. There was still the habitual lack of openness between us, exacerbated by their unwillingness to learn about my trust in God, and so, with great effort, I concealed my illness from them. However, one morning, my dad, who had kept me at a distance and said many terrible things over the past years, couldn't wait for me to come down to breakfast. When I sat at my place, I saw that he had tucked £200 beside my plate! Peace in our family was restored. While Dad never made it to Africa on his travels around the world, he would, after this, enquire about my work, and Dad and Mum even ended up supporting several students who were learning seamstress skills through a programme Caroline and I had set up.

Eventually, I decided a term back at ANCC would be helpful in my recuperation. I was blessed to have John, my old tutor, and a thoroughly restful time attending only whatever lectures I wanted.

It was also during this time that Great Aunt Nan died. She was a kind, gentle friend over the years and a good sounding board for family concerns. The last time I'd really conversed with her was in her own wee bungalow in Newton Stewart in southwest Scotland. We agreed that we had been good friends and said our fond farewells. The next time I came to the UK she was still physically in good shape, but her memory was gone. She was moved to Cumloden Manor Nursing Home and I visited her, but she didn't know who I was unless I constantly reminded her.

I prayed that, despite her being in care and showing signs of dementia, she wouldn't die until she accepted Jesus. She lingered on until I realised that God loved her more than I did, and only He knew the true state of her heart, so I released her into His plans and she passed away very soon. In discussions with Dad she had said that she didn't want a funeral, but my parents felt uncomfortable cremating her without someone saying something. They asked me, as the Christian in the family, to take the funeral. I was still very ill but managed a short, meaningful service. This led to Dad asking me to do his funeral too.

It's interesting how even people who have no time for God in their normal lives see the need for His comfort and reality when sorrow strikes. This was one way in which they saw my faith intersecting with their point of need, and I was grateful both for how it spoke of an inner need for God deep inside their hearts, and a further assurance of my dad's love and trust in me.

CHAPTER 12

RETURN TO AFRICA

After nine months off I was keen to get back to my home in Tanzania to resume work. When I arrived I was still shaky and fatigued, but very thankful for having staff to do the jobs that I didn't need to do like shopping, cooking, housework and gardening. This freed me up to do my own job, but I went back to work gradually and I did what I could and then rested. This proved to be the best plan for recovery – not full but good. Five to seven hours a day seemed quite respectable and there were still the usual lunchtime visitors at home. This gave me a routine and at least I could feel that I was achieving something, which was important.

While I was away there was quite a bit of trouble in the various ministries with which I had been involved, with some serious results, and I was very glad that I wasn't there to get caught up in the politics. I returned after the dust had settled, having made no enemies.

While working part-time in the Dodoma hangar I got unofficial news that the current Chad engineer was leaving and, despite my poor health, I felt God stir me to go again to help out. Looking around the programme, I was the only person with the qualifications, experience and availability to go. Based on my previous experience of the Chad hangar, I felt it expedient to offer my services on the condition that I could take someone to help for a few weeks until I got the hangar under control. So, a few weeks later Heri, a language school teacher whom we had recruited as an engineer because of his integrity and ability to learn, headed for Chad with me.

The hangar and aircraft were showing signs of neglect, and the pilots had not enjoyed good relationships with the mechanic. I was glad of Heri's help as we slogged away and made lots of improvements over the six weeks he was there. After work Heri liked to go to one of the local hotels for a swim. I would sit by the pool in my sweaty dungarees and steel-toed work boots reading the aircraft manual as I've never been a fan of swimming.

Once, early on, Heri was targeted because of his black skin. I was driving him back to the TEAM compound across town after dinner on the MAF compound. He did not have his passport or a certified copy of it on him. The soldiers shouted at him in French and, in my poor French/Arabic lingo, I tried to explain that he didn't understand French.

'But he's black. He must speak French!' they argued.

'But he's from Tanzania. They don't speak French there!'

We stayed calm and polite, but because we showed no sign of paying a bribe, they eventually took him out of the pickup and started to march him down the road. In my head I was praying fervently and wondering what to do when suddenly Heri was back in the car. The drunken, armed soldiers saw us as a waste of time. One made a final attempt to extract some money by leaning through the driver's window, fingering my Chadian driving licence. I told him to keep it. He threw it on my lap and angrily told us to go.

In the daytime, travel across town was punctuated by stops at temporary police checkpoints. Armed and stroppy, they checked light bulbs, the fire extinguisher, paperwork, driving licence, and anything else they could think of – and it didn't matter if you passed through the same checkpoint several times in the space of a few hours, they always stopped you and did the same checks.

I once made the mistake of ignoring an officer who was two exits further around a roundabout from the one I was taking. He waved, but I wasn't sure that it was at me, and I would have had to go further around the roundabout to get to him, so I just carried on. He pursued me on a moped and forced me to go back. No matter how polite and contrite I was, and despite the fact that there were no faulty bulbs, fire extinguishers or paperwork, he wanted money. I left him my driving licence. Evariste, the MAF Office Manager, who had been a police officer, went to HQ to get it back. He had friends in high places and got it without having to pay anything, with the officer involved getting a bit of flack from his superior. Smarting with wounded pride, on the way out of the office, he told Evariste that he would be watching out for me and that next time I would pay. Thankfully we never met again, but I did have some uneasy moments wondering if we would.

The Toy Boy resumed his unsought courtship. In the years since I'd left Chad he had managed to have an illegitimate baby with a French expat, who wanted nothing more to do with him and moved back to France. He came almost every day to press his suit, showing me pictures of his cute offspring and making it clear that he would like to repeat the exercise with me. He was, at least, a good source of local information and gossip.

Every day, during certain months of the year, a nomad lady would walk past the hangar with a large round gourd held by leather strips on her back. One day the Toy Boy was sitting on a chair as I was working on an aircraft.

'Have you ever tried camel milk?' he asked.

'No!'

Next thing he had summoned the nomad lady and bought four litres which we boiled up in an old Nido tin in a kettle of water. While we were waiting we had a conversation with Hawa (Eve in English). The Toy Boy, interpreting, said that she had noticed me and knew that I was a woman even though I was doing a man's job. She thought I must, therefore, be rich and could afford at least two husbands. She also asked for an old oil-drum to cut in half lengthways for watering her camels. I was able to give her one and, by way of thanks, she brought me a smaller version of the gourd she carried (I still have it, and the inside still smells of camel milk), and invited me to her camp in the bush. Some days later Daniel and I drove there.

Hawa graciously welcomed us into her tent; long, thin blackened tree roots tied with fine strips of leather formed an ovoid frame, over which strips of kanga material and grass mats were draped. The side strips could be rolled up to allow air to circulate. The camel saddles sat at the ends and served as storage. The bed was four flat X-shaped planks with a delicate-looking mat of twigs and leather strips. We sat on mats on the sandy floor, which was carefully contoured to prevent any rainwater ingress. Adorable baby camels in shades of chocolate, fawn, and white wandered around the camp waiting for their mothers to come back from a watering hole. Neighbours rode up, tied their horses to any convenient tree branch, and came in to discuss the weather.

We had many small but strong cups of freshly brewed sweet coffee and crispy bits of fried pastry and dried dates. The men allowed us to show the Jesus Film in the camp for all the neighbours (Jesus is also an important figure for Muslims). Only men were allowed, but the women may have watched secretly from a distance. The men greatly appreciated the film. 'Please come again!' they said. 'And could we see a film of Saddam Hussein too?'

Since I knew that Hawa didn't have a tarpaulin for her tent, I brought her one on my second visit and she, by way of thanks, gave me her two solid silver rings, which amounted to the contents of her entire bank account. It was a friendship of equals.

When the rains came she and her family left for the north to avoid the excess water that brings insects that bite camels, causing them to sicken and die. By the time she came back, seven months later, I had returned to Tanzania. I have never

Gathering around the table in Norway on a sheep-shearing trip during my high school years. My dad, Billy, is second from the left.

Me and Dad – often at odds, yet so much alike.

A youthful portrait with one of my dearest friends.

Having a great time at work on the base in Dodoma.
(Courtesy of MAF.)

Hanging in the hangar with Ruth McKelvey, a dear teacher friend. She inhabited the other half of my semi-detached house on the MAF base.

'Auntie' Caroline with Maasai warriors.
(Courtesy of Caroline Ackerman Marschall.)

Enjoying a visit with Caroline's dogs.
(Courtesy of Caroline Ackerman Marschall.)

*Can you see the resemblance? Me with
Ruth Kambenga, my spiritual twin.*
(Courtesy of Ruth Kambenga.)

Pastor Dismus and his wife Martha.
(Courtesy of Caroline Ackerman Marschall.)

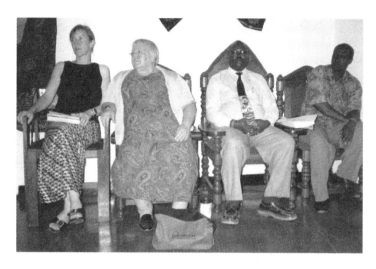

An action shot of me, Caroline, Dismus, and an elder in a church service.

Blending in!

The Toy Boy

Caught off guard, lounging atop Matilda with dogs Hector and Bracken.

Cajoled into posing alongside one of my house guards!

A happy day with Mr Conn.
(Reproduced with the kind permission of Ken Pearson,
photographer in Stranraer, Scotland.)

With Dismus and Martha on my only visit to Tanzania after leaving the mission field. Dismus proudly sports a Scottish 'See you, Jimmy' hat!

Having some cold fun on one of our mini-honeymoons in Vienna.

Watching the world go by on an American train.

Neil Conn on Annie's bench in rural Galloway.
(Courtesy of Neil MacLeod.)

forgotten this beautiful lady with her incense-infused skin. This friendship, at least, was one thing for which I could thank the Toy Boy.

Daniel once said with great enthusiasm, 'You're such a great boss' (here I started to feel good about myself), 'you could make work for a hundred people!' Indeed, the hangar staff worked very hard. The folks in the adjoining hangars commented on how well and hard we worked as a team but, as much as they admired the results, they were not prepared to follow suit.

The Aero club was run by, and for, some very self-assured Frenchmen who were based in N'Djamena. They did not have a mechanic and often used the watchmen to carry out repairs. I stayed as far away as possible, as getting sucked into what was basically an illegal operation was not the way to keep my licence or keep others safe. However, the watchmen often popped round to borrow many of the things lacking in their hangar or for help understanding the English manuals.

On one memorable occasion, they needed to borrow a stand that should have been used merely to prop up a wing while taking out its supporting strut. I peered around our wall to see that they had jacked the stand up so high that the wing was pushed up at a crazy angle and the upper surface of the fuselage was wrinkled. I had spent a long time, and much effort, getting all of our equipment calibrated (not easy in such a remote location), and a posse of oversized, huffing and puffing Aero club members then came to ask if they could use the pitot static tester, which checks basic instrumentation. They really did treat me as if I was a tool waitress!

However, I was unwilling for my equipment to be misused, so I agreed to carry out an unofficial test. I knew that these chaps had no confidence in a woman mechanic, but I pressed on. There was a huge leak in the system and I explained that it could take time to find. They rolled their eyes and puffed some more as if to say, 'Just what we expected of an incompetent woman!' I prayed fervently, 'Please God, don't humble me in front of these arrogant men!' I took one panel off and found the leak. It certainly took the wind out of their sails.

After Heri left I had a short visit from another Tanzanian hangar assistant, Ben Kulwa, but his six-week stint was interrupted by the death of his father. Soon I was alone in the hangar with the lovely but hazardous Daniel, a hangar guard, and whatever visitors (or potential baby-daddies) passed by. The benefit of having more than one engineer is enormous. Working alone requires even more attention to detail and precision. Items that need double checks mean doing a job and then walking away and coming back with a fresh pair of eyes.

My responsibilities did not end with servicing the planes as a number of common-sense issues simply seemed not to occur to the nationals. There was a lot of long grass outside the hangar next to the taxiway and the guards from the other hangars used to disappear into it with their water-filled bright plastic kettles to relieve themselves and, as a result, we were inundated with flies. I got our guards to cut a lot of grass so they had to go further to do their stuff, and hoped that the flies wouldn't commute. It seemed to work.

I was invited on a village trip by Limane from our office. I had not had a day off for many weeks. In Tanzania, I spent many weekends in villages, so I was glad to accept. We set off on a Friday evening in a small car in intense heat. The road surfaces were broken up into amazingly uniform cubes of tarmac, so much swerving was required. Smoother sand roads led us into the village. We were sweaty and, as ever, the great hospitality of our hosts led them to offer water, which would have been carried from a distant water hole for us to wash in. I was ushered into a mud room in the square enclosed compound. The 'shower', as usual, was a bucket of warm water and a stone emerging from a patch of mud. The stench of human waste was almost overpowering. I thought I had better use the loo first, so that, if there was unavoidable contact with human waste, at least I would have the chance to clean up. I asked

Limane where the loo was and he sheepishly told me that it had become full and been capped off. I guessed that, given the smell, it was the room where my washing water was. He said I could go behind a bush outside the compound. It was after dark and there was only one small bush. As I was wearing my baggy boubou which, carefully draped, could protect one's modesty without getting polluted, the task was accomplished, but I was acutely aware that a white bottom would be a source of fascination to the nationals.

When travelling, my digestive system has consistently been lazy. This has the benefit of being able to travel far without the need for 'facilities', but as lots of food is often part of village visits, it can also be uncomfortable, eventually requiring attention. After wonderful fellowship, we all slept under the trees on mattresses. Again, the boubou was invaluable as bedclothes. Early on the Sunday morning I awoke and my stomach was swollen. So, having taken a Senokot and with much prayer, I quietly did sit-ups whilst the others slept. Finally, there were signs of a result, so I got up and went out to find a quiet spot just as ladies were up brushing the rubbish off their dusty yards. I wandered out of the village and finally found a small patch of dry grass long enough to give me some shelter. Satisfyingly, all worked well, and I was praising God when my thoughts were interrupted by a rustling in the grass behind me. The moment ruined, I turned to see a small black pig in the grass eyeballing me intensely. Being bitten by a pig in such a remote and hot place would have been life-threatening, but being a farmer's daughter used to animals, I finished what I was doing, then slowly stood up and moved away. There was another rustle and then a chomping noise. The pig had come to eat my work, and followed me home hoping for more. Not much is wasted in the bush!

After my year and a week on the second trip to Chad, the previous MAF mechanic returned and I went back to Tanzania. Just before I left I was offered a new role in MAF Tanzania that would have suited me very well; however, I felt uneasy. I had committed to the MAF engineering team for as long as they needed me, so to test this, I emailed my Tanzania boss. He told me I was still needed full-time in the hangar, so I turned down the new job. This made me unpopular with some of the MAF Tanzania team who felt that it was my duty to accept and a couple of people tried to change my decision, but I held my ground.

I resumed my role as Hangar Foreman in MAF Tanzania, and I was made Assistant Pastor at church and started village ministry with Ruth again. But, with the passing of time, it was getting harder with the ME and I had to force myself to maintain the required standards. I was becoming ready to move on.

CHAPTER 13

KLM: EVANGELIST TO THE VILLAGES

Based on Ruth's and my expanding ministry in rural areas, I had a strong desire to work in village evangelism full-time. Mr Kiroge, the TCAA Inspector, once reminded me that, when I first arrived in Tanzania, I had told him that I would work at MAF for 10 years. I exceeded that commitment by the space of one week.

Through hard work and transparency, Dismus and I had been successful in turning around our local church and area. He was voted Head of the whole denomination of KLM Tanzania, and he headhunted me to resurrect the Department of Evangelism. It was my dream job and it came at just the right time. Working under the leadership of Dismus was also a dream. He looked after me well but also gave me freedom, even to make mistakes.

There was the question of where to live and, as I did not want to continue living on MAF Compound 'A', I started looking around hoping, particularly, for a house near Ruth. Three people separately took me to see the same house that had been on the market for years. It was the same distance away from Ruth's house as the MAF compound. Legally it would be difficult for a person not fully resident in Tanzania to purchase, but I felt God tell me to buy it.

It was only £14,000 and I had money from Aunt Nan, but had never touched it so as not to antagonise Dad any more than necessary. So I said to God, 'If you want me to buy this house, then Dad has to agree.' I discussed it with him and, at first, he was quite negative, but all of a sudden he said, 'Oh well, let's do it! If things go wrong, it's not as if I haven't made mistakes in the past.' I was gobsmacked. It was another solid sign that his anger toward me was melting.

Major repairs had to be done. New roof, new electrics, water storage system, veranda, guards' hut and shower, kennels, and a new perimeter wall. I felt that last one was an unnecessary expense, but Ruth's husband Henry built it as a replacement for the old fence and presented me with a bill for a million shillings, payment needed immediately. I didn't have it but was committed to making sure everything was paid on time. I wanted the new home to be blessed and for everyone who worked on it to have good experiences. Dad called me that evening to say that some shares had been cashed in compulsorily – and the amount being paid was the pound equivalent of the required million shillings! As it happened, I was very glad in the years to come for the privacy that the wall gave.

It turned out that the neighbours had been using the septic tanks in the garden, and they were already full. One of them even had half his tank in our garden. We removed all of the tanks and rerouted the sewage into the municipal system, and I insisted that the half tank be removed. The owner claimed that they had not plumbed into my old system, but in fact tree roots were blocking his own pipes, which we fixed several times at our own expense. Years later, when his tenants caused problems, he tried to get me to pay for repairs, but I refused even to speak to him about any compensation. It was his own fault for lying and we had done a great deal more for him than might be expected.

Finally, two months of frantic activity involving extensive repairs and hordes of labourers culminated in moving into a habitable house of great character (i.e. many faults) with great potential (i.e. possibly some of the faults could be fixed). I cannot say that I was sad to be leaving MAF, as my home was a five-minute leisurely stroll from the hangar and I expected to see my old workmates regularly as Dodoma was a small town.

Everybody says, 'Oh, we'll miss you!' but in the day-to-day busyness, people are forgotten a week or two after they have left the team and are remembered only when something crops up with which they had associations. For example, departing missionaries often leave their clothes behind for others to buy, and I felt very cross once when I observed a Korean lady wearing one of Ruth McKelvey's dresses after she went home – I felt it should have been my old friend back. However, I wasn't going far away, and was invited to come back to clean up the hangar whenever I felt like it! And I did indeed continue to work for them from time to time on a voluntary basis.

In a practical sense, however, leaving the MAF compound after ten years was a bit like a teenager leaving home. Moving to a private residence meant I had to deal with things that had been provided automatically on the established MAF compound. Because of the high risk of aggravated burglaries, and for the sake of the guard dogs, it was wise to have a watchman on site at all times. I kept on Mzee (Old Man) Said, who had been employed under appalling terms by the previous owner – 24 hours a day, 7 days a week for only a day's wages – and three others were also hired. I had two Catholics who could work weekday/night shifts with Sundays off for Mass, one Seventh Day Adventist (Paulo, whose parents were both lepers in the village at Hombolo hospital), who had Saturdays off, and Said, as a Muslim, had Friday off. The reasoning was that no one had the excuse that they were being kept from worship.

Shifts were scheduled, the pay well above the minimum wage set annually by the Tanzanian government, and they were encouraged to join the Union. I was glad of the Union rep when Mzee took to drink and turned up very squiffy, which would, of course, be dangerous if any thieves arrived. He had to be warned by the rep and then dismissed officially following Tanzanian employment laws. Sadly, I believe that his problem came about because of having a bigger wage and much more free time, so in a way my exceeding the government standards backfired.

We also signed up for pension contributions, which gave them 'free' medical care (deducted from their contributions, but helpful nonetheless). As I understand, we were the first employer in Dodoma to do so. Shamefully, as far as I know, most of the other relatively well-off expats who employed domestic staff never engaged with the official employment establishment. Because their workers didn't get their rights, they ended up borrowing from their employers – which always caused complications. As a 'newbie' I had adopted this approach too, but eventually found a more formal position worked better.

The guards were supplemented by a handsome Rhodesian Ridgeback pup called Bracken, who at six months old weighed in at 24kg, ate more than two people, and promised to be a formidable deterrent to thieves. My cat Nyau, however, had him under her not so delicate little paw. My little flock of hens had been rehomed as Bracken's hunting instincts got too much for him and wholesale slaughter was only narrowly avoided.

When I was a child I had a dog – Pip – whom I loved so much that it translated into a deep love for all dogs, and indeed all animals (chickens not excluded). Throughout my life I had rarely been without some form of pets, whether cats, dogs, farm animals, and even pet rats which built themselves a Smaug-like palace of torn tissues and cloths in my room, unbeknown to my Aberdeen landlady. Where I couldn't own a dog, I had actively developed relationships with other people's through house or dog-sitting. So, as you can imagine, Bracken was infinitely more than just a guard dog. He was, in fact, one of the most loved animals I ever had, and a new member of my family.

I asked the watchmen what they needed to feel safe in addition to our large fierce dog and a very bright flashlight, and they asked for a bow and arrows. Mzee Said bought some without poison, as I had insisted. A poison arrow would kill eventually.

Better an arrow in the rear than death! However, I found Francis 'improving' them with new flights and massive barbed tips. One night a thief came over the fence and Francis was about to shoot him but Bracken got to him first and chased him away. After this incident, spikes were added to the top of the boundary walls, except where the watchmen could climb over into our neighbour's garden to raise the alarm. Their written contract stated that risking being overpowered and possibly killed was not to be contemplated or even helpful.

Many of the original plants of our small village churches had been set up by missionaries who liked hunting, and so often these churches were in remote areas. They were generally organised in groups under an elected Area Leader. I had found that spending time face to face is necessary to really touch base meaningfully with people. I would head off in Matilda and visit at least four adjacent 'Areas' for a week each before returning to Dodoma. And so began three years of spending at least eight months a year in villages. For me, it was a dream come true.

As a well-established person, I was in a strong position to welcome small groups from the West, organise activities, with Tanzanian nationals, and I was also able to help Auntie Caroline with her teams from the USA, usually as a driver, interpreter and general gofer. It was hard work making the trips safe and meaningful for the teams and the nationals with whom they came into contact. Even if Westerners seemed willing in mind and spirit to adapt to African village ways, despite having the basics explained and having agreed to do everything in their power to accommodate, most just couldn't.

Unfamiliar food prepared and served in unhygienic conditions by Western standards would be a prime example. So many promised to eat everything they were given, understanding that refusing can be very offensive to a host with limited resources, only to stubbornly refuse to eat anything when a meal was served. There are a number of ways to politely avoid eating in villages. One time I had hit my head, resulting in a headache, and made that an excuse not to eat a meal of rancid goat meat. My favoured option was to point to someone more deserving of respect than myself, and to announce that they really should have the greatest delicacies, such as eyeballs. This often worked in a society so sensitive to hierarchy. Another friend made a point of fasting while she was on village visits, as the tribal respect for spiritual customs meant they wouldn't press you to eat.

Thankfully, I was able to help the guests and smooth over things with the hosts with effusive apologies and explanations. It was very hard work and took every cross-cultural and linguistic skill I had picked up over the years to make sure that there were still positive experiences for all involved.

Another frequent difficulty was dress code. In the West, people going to the countryside often dress casually and wear trainers. For an event, turning up on time is seen as the critical way to show respect. In contrast, African people often live in deep poverty and yet dress very smartly to honour an occasion. Arriving late is seldom a problem, and the greater the importance of the guest, the later they can arrive as long as they have dressed well. Smart, shiny shoes are important despite the dust and dirt underfoot; and yet nearly all Westerners would turn up casually dressed. It was understandable as we often travelled in my battered old Land Rover on rough or sand roads to bush villages, visiting poor people living in dusty mud huts and probably staying in tents. But their 'practical' wear was not always appreciated.

Part of success in ministry was keeping the right priorities. For one week, I led a team ministering in a village which was some two hours into the bush from Dodoma. World Vision had worked there for years and the Tanzanian lady who was in charge of the project was very excited when she heard we were coming. She said that they had made a big mistake by promoting small projects, in an attempt to reduce poverty, more than the gospel. She had learned an important truth and reminded me of it; if people are not transformed by the Word of God, even the small projects don't succeed.

CHAPTER 14

FARU

As Head of the Department of Evangelism for KLM la Tanzania, I was tasked with developing and overseeing the evangelism work of the denomination on a country-wide level. This would cover a network of approximately 300 churches and around 30,000 members. Tanzania had some completely unreached people groups, and my aim was to equip churches and individuals to reach the lost across the country. I was to strengthen churches in an apostolic role, liaising with church leadership to help bring about accountability, financial responsibility, envisioning, and godly governance. This would involve running seminars, courses, conferences and lectures on various key issues to strengthen churches and prepare them to receive new converts, and most importantly, develop an evangelism strategy that nationals could deliver without dependence on outside help.

Dismus insisted that I be ordained to give me some authority and further decreed I wear a black dress, which I did – paired with a bright green jacket printed with a blue striped zebra. Always a rebel at heart! I promised that I would pastor every person without prejudice, and I have endeavoured to do so and be a blessing to everyone I made contact with since that promise was made, even after the end of that ministry.

However, I did get the name *Faru* (Rhino or military tank for heavy warfare) because very often, on our travels, it was clear that those who had put themselves forward as leaders were doing woefully poorly and were unrepentant when challenged. It needed clarity of communication, assertiveness and sometimes force to deal with issues arising.

I had little sympathy with unrepentant leaders. The Bible says that a teacher will be judged more harshly. A leader should do everything in their power to live a transparent life of integrity. Dismus knew my attitude toward such people and I could not and still do not believe that it is right to defend and conceal unrighteous attitudes and behaviours in church leaders. These things need to be exposed and appropriate action taken to protect the members affected, ensuring that the cause of Christ is not opened to scorn.

One issue was that many of our pastors were not actually married to their partners, or had had only a traditional rather than a legal ceremony. An edict was sent out from HQ that they should rectify the situation within a given period of time. Sadly, one of the missionaries had confused her culture with Christianity and was bringing white wedding dresses and veils in. Some people refused to get married without these accoutrements, thinking that they legitimised the ceremony, when they were simply fashions that came in with Queen Victoria!

Life in Dodoma was rich, varied and involved a lot of learning and relying on God to guide. There were seldom simple solutions, so thinking deeply through issues kept one's mind alive and alert. This gave me a great interest in theology and culturally appropriate responses rather than imposing my own preconceived ideas.

We had long serious discussions with the leadership team. Part of the need I saw was for external accountability for their local situations. Traditional missionaries have frequently imposed culturally appropriate interpretations from their own countries of origin but, instead, we agreed that, by listening and facilitating thoughts and discussions, we would help them interpret the scriptures in a way that reflected their cultures. The best example was from a newly evangelised area, where their questions were wonderfully practical, along the lines of 'Is it permissible to eat with someone who has been accused of witchcraft?'

Another, particularly complicated, query was this:

'If an old man dies, his four eldest sons slaughter a cow (by holding its nose and smothering it, as traditions need the blood) and smear half of the father's corpse with fat taken from the cow's insides. The corpse is buried wrapped in the skin and the meat is served to those who come to the funeral. Can one do this as a Christian?'

To answer this, it is essential to understand what these rituals mean in context. Are they part of Tambiko? This is a blood sacrifice made to placate the spirit of the deceased which, if unsatisfied, will vent its fury by causing misfortune and disaster on the living who showed disrespect and will have to be identified by consulting a witch doctor and then be placated at great cost. Or, is it just a culturally appropriate show of respect for an elder? They didn't know, so I arranged for my theologically educated, wise Maasai friend in Dodoma, Paul Sandamu, to visit and help them decide.

Basically, if it was just respect, however strange it might seem to others, why should they not continue? If Tambiko, then as Christians believing that Jesus' blood is the last blood sacrifice that should be availed upon, they would not continue. Paul went some weeks later and helped them to come to their conclusions. It was Tambiko.

I asked to run some seminars for our Bible students in Babati, and we had very lively discussions on a number of issues in the church including the dangers of following the trends and fashions in Christianity without understanding the relevant Biblical principles involved. One example would be the use of 'Praise the Lord,' to which the appropriate rejoinder is 'Amen/ Amina.' This is misused in the following ways:

1. To test if someone is born again – if they don't say Amen, then apparently, they aren't!
2. To get people to be quiet because, if they have to say Amen, they can't be talking about other things.
3. Someone who has a badly prepared/unprepared message will say it so often that any message there was gets lost.

I also talked to them about how to cast out evil spirits in a wise way and how to test prophecy (there was a lot of false prophecy around!), and I asked the final year students to consider giving themselves to pastor churches in areas of great need.

The previous missionaries who had lived and worked in the villages had done a good job regarding polygamy. Many Westerners may be surprised to learn that the Bible comes down harder on divorce than polygamy – though provision is made for both. Maasai families arrange marriages for their children with desirable connections as soon as they are born. When a Maasai warrior stops his nomadic wanderings, he comes home to become an elder and then takes the wives as prearranged. However, the Bible says anyone in eldership in a church should have only one wife. Obviously, when the new church was set up, those who were responsible and respected enough to be church elders already had several wives. So, the understanding was that elders should not add to the wives they already had (Daniel M said he was glad he already had his four, with two looking after the maize fields and goats in bush farmsteads, one the cows, and the youngest his townhouse, before becoming an elder. At great cost in cows he paid off the fathers of the others to whom he had been promised). One of their number had taken another wife and was removed from his position. The young ones coming up agreed not to take more than one wife.

This had caused Makarote a perplexing issue. As a young man, he had not married before going to the Babati Bible School and returning to be the pastor. An unmarried man, or one with few wives, can be seen as weak – he was. In addition, which one of his many potential affianced brides should he choose, and which should he pay off? He made an unwise choice and ended up with a sulky millstone around his neck. But it was his right to choose, and that, I felt, needed to be respected.

During a weekend of seminars in a village, we were talking to a church member when she confessed to sleeping with the pastor. We called him in and he admitted it and agreed to put his life right. His wife had left him ten years before, but in our evening film showing, she felt God tell her to go back to him. A few weeks later we returned to the village to bless their marriage again.

In addition, the painful issue of female genital mutilation was tackled. This barbaric traditional practice is often carried out by parents wanting the best marriage prospects for their daughters and could be interpreted as a loving act in this context. The older men with young daughters said that they would agree not to subject their girls to FGM *if* those with eligible sons and the unmarried Christian men would agree to marry them.

It is very difficult to run a denomination successfully (by Western standards) without decent procedures and disciplines. Many of our colleagues in Tanzania didn't have the education or experience to equip them for such a task. Missionaries come and go and set up 'necessary' Western systems that never work properly in their absence because there is no understanding of why they are necessary and what they are meant to achieve! The same is true for government offices and offices of utilities, which are bound by many procedures that have departed from their original intention so far as to make dealings with them deeply frustrating, thereby presenting the very real temptation to use bribes to bypass the unusable systems. Most African churches depend heavily on outside funding and are forced to comply with systems to satisfy the demands of the sponsors, who themselves are governed by increasingly tight legislation in their own countries. It is not easy for anyone involved. Most, if not all, of the complications revolve around money.

Even the church leadership was used to holding people to lesser account when it came to finances. One village church started to think of ideas for developing their outreach, which was enormously encouraging. But when Dismus visited the church, he said the people, although they had been willing to invest in their future, didn't need to give anything themselves. They were too poor. When we left the village, Caroline took him aside and told him he was ruining everything. 'If the people can do something, they are not poor,' she told him. 'Poor is a mindset. You came from this village and used to live like these people. Now you're in Dodoma, and you have a nice home and luxuries, but these people don't have that. And if they don't start working for themselves and giving to their own church, they won't have anything.'

Occasionally, as Westerners, Caroline and I got away with rebuking men in authority in a way that a national woman wouldn't have dreamed of doing. But we did not abuse this position and indeed showed as much respect for our male leaders as we could.

We went to deal with the case of a pastor in the Manyara area who had a complaint against his Area Leader after being disciplined, he felt, unfairly. There was a long and involved history including, but not exclusively based on, the rather interesting way he and the church choir had raised funds for some much coveted guitars. The usual way is to have a Harambee, where on a set day the church members, plus friends and as many influential (and more importantly rich) people as possible, gather and money is given publicly, either willingly or extracted by teasing or shaming people.

Sometimes they are great fun and other times downright embarrassing, but one constant is that those asking other people to contribute must first show their commitment by giving a considerable sum. Without this nobody else will consider supporting them in any way. The pastor and his choir did not have money, so they borrowed some from someone in the village, divided it amongst themselves, and in the Harambee went forward to give it as if it was their own. The money was counted, the final amount announced and prayed for, and then afterward they subtracted the loaned sum and returned it to the chap who had lent it to them.

In effect, they had deceived the community and, as in all villages where secrets are few and far between, this was widely known.

The Area Committee were clearly sure that the representatives sent by the General Assembly (i.e. myself and two others) had already decided against them beforehand, so they were very aggressive. The pastor was confident that he would be reinstated once all the facts had been heard, but, just in case, he had summoned the choir and others not involved in the meeting to be outside the church to defend him...possibly with violence if it came to it, which thankfully it didn't!

As it was, we had to go with the Area Leader's decision to remove him from his position. We talked and prayed with him alone, then with him and his wife, then with the choir and the church elders, trying to salvage what we could. In the end, the pastor refused to be disciplined and the following Sunday summoned the church to meet at his house. More than half came to the normal service in the church instead, and I discussed with them what should be done. It was encouraging to see them choosing to forgive freely, and one man who had stopped coming to church because of the pastor's behaviour came for the first time in years.

I spent one lunchtime break talking to an elder in a Barabaig church. The Barabaig are considered the scum of Tanzania. They are very easy to spot because of their traditional clothes (shiny brass coils around necks, arms and legs, tatted goatskin skirts), hairstyles (a ball of hair on the back of the skull, the front shaved), smell (they use *samli*, a kind of butter made from rancid milk, all over their bodies), and very specific markings on their faces (lots of small scars circling the eyes, making them look somewhat owlish). If cattle are stolen they are the first suspects. They are also well known as witch doctors, notoriously resistant to the Gospel because of the strong hold their dark culture has on them and because of their nomadic lifestyle and exclusion from society. If a Barabaig converts, it is considered to be a major miracle.

We had a few small Barabaig churches. We were discussing the whole issue of names and clothing, and I was lamenting the fact that when they convert they leave off wearing their traditional clothes, wear western clothes and take new Biblical names. In the West we are always being reminded of how much better it is to leave people their own culture as much as possible. However, in this case, my western sensibilities were misleading.

This man, in typical African fashion, first gave me a living example; he asked me if I'd ever seen the Barabaig goats and cows. Their skins are heavily scarred with complex, and sometimes very beautiful, artwork so that it is easy to identify which animal belongs to which family. It is impossible to steal them unless you kill and dispose of the evidence before you are caught. These marks are about ownership. He then went on to explain that, in the same way, if a Christian Barabaig even wears just a traditional bracelet, never mind the full garb, the message to the others is that he has not actually made a real break from tradition; he still belongs. It is very important for a Barabaig to have the outward signs of conversion to avoid giving the wrong message. That certainly gave me a lot to think about.

On one occasion, we officiated at the wedding of a pastor to the mother of his children. She caused a bit of a stir by having her hair long and plaited, Swahili style, in contrast to the shaven heads of the traditional ladies. To them it was nothing short of a woman dressing as a man, as in Maasai tradition it is only the young warriors who have long plaited hair. Anyway, it was her choice, it was her own culture she was challenging, and it was her wedding. Her husband was proud to be breaking with tradition to be faithful to one woman.

I believe we taught our people ways of right thinking rather than pat answers. We were often asked to arbitrate in long-standing difficult situations that had developed within churches, and I also like to think we spread a gentle wisdom and true peace to our members.

CHAPTER 15

VILLAGE PEOPLE

Living in villages so much had its challenges. It was always an adventure, for instance, discovering where one was assigned to sleep. It was assumed that I would be lonely sleeping on my own and so if Ruth wasn't there I would be given a room with one or more girls. Some had worrying coughs that could have been TB, and to be honest I would have preferred a bit of alone time just to prepare for the intense pastoring required by those we were visiting. Beds could be cow skins or mattresses (one had little maggots in it). And in one place they gave me and Ruth a bed in a room that had been used to store corpses. They gave it to us because it was a room that commanded respect, but it smelled so bad that I really couldn't stay. I considered sleeping under a nearby tree, but thankfully the men had a spare room in their lodgings and we made the excuse that it was easier for us all to stay together.

Washing facilities were usually a bucket of water and a stone to stand on. The size and stability of stones varied, and often they were located on a patch of muddy ground, so care was needed to avoid getting dirtier. Toilets were usually long drops. Not all users aimed well, and not all toilets had safe coverings to stand on, so one had to survey the floor well and tread carefully and make sure that car keys were safely stowed and not in danger of tumbling into the pit of no return! On one occasion, this actually

109

happened. I felt greatly for the local man who volunteered for a rescue mission!

On one medical trip with Auntie Caroline in Arusha, we went to meet up with the missionaries and choir ladies from the new Maasai Church in Gelai. We were all staying in a guesthouse with the rooms opening onto the courtyard. It had been a busy day and we went to bed weary. Caroline ordered a cup of tea, which a waitress brought on a tray to be picked up the next morning. In the early hours I awoke to hear Caroline wondering, 'Where are my teeth?' As the junior, and fitter, partner in this outfit, I realised my duty and got up to search our room. Then it occurred to me that maybe the teeth had been put in a teacup on the now absent tray. After several minutes of grubbing in the kitchen waste – think heat, rot and flies – I found them. Stoic Caroline just cleaned them off and put them in.

On this trip I saw Caroline in action. Looby, a local guy, had a nasty boil on his thigh. She stuck a big bore needle deep into it, stirred it around, and then tried to squeeze out pus – none came out, but the whole procedure was a cringe. Years later I asked Looby about it. Typical Maasai, taught not to react to pain, he denied any suffering!

Ruth Kambenga and I were in a village one time, teaching seminars, and after the service we returned to the pastor's house. On entering I encountered a strong and foul smell not unlike that of human faeces. I've had it on my shoes before and so did a quick check...nothing! The smell diminished but returned with the food that was put before us at lunchtime. The hostess, who is a dear friend, removed the covers from the dishes, revealing dagaa (small sun-dried fish much like whitebait). I thought that maybe my smell receptors had been giving false information – dagaa stinks, but not that badly! However, the first mouthful confirmed the worst; they were completely rotten.

It is important to note that village pastors have a very low standard of living and seldom, if ever, have the luxury of choosing what they eat. It was clear that these dear people had nothing else and that the problem was probably that my friend had cooked the dagaa well in advance so that she would have time to sit and chat (a luxury which pastors' wives seldom have as they are usually busy in the kitchen). So, saying a quick and heartfelt prayer, I set to and finished my share without a grimace or a retch – which was in itself miraculous – and I am pleased to say that no tummy upset resulted. This has to be the worst meal I have ever had, and as it was eaten using hands, the foul smell lingered there for quite some time!

Other times we met with unexpected luxury. Up near Lake Natron, about four hours' drive north of Arusha, through a hunting area, a team of KLM missionaries had built a base near Gelai. One Christmas Auntie Caroline and I went to visit. We were picked up by Moose, who drove us from the main paved road, through deep foliage in the gloriously flowering meadows of the bush that threatened to clog the radiator, along riverbeds, and across screes of tyre-challenging volcanic pebbles.

We arrived and found an amazing home complete with a Christmas tree and large freezer full of American fare – they had three teenage daughters and were mindful of the sacrifices these girls had made to allow their parents to be in Gelai, including attending boarding school near Nairobi. This was the first of several stays I had there.

One year I took Dismus and Sanka, a self-made man, to facilitate their roles. Sanka's story is a good one, worth retelling here. He was the youngest son of the seventh and youngest wife of a man wealthy in cows. When his father died his elder brothers sold off the livestock and squandered the money on drink. Sanka worked to pay for his schooling, put himself through school and was so thrifty with any earnings that, by the time I got to know him as General Treasurer for KLM Tanzania, he was the owner of a farmstead at Suum, a big townhouse in Mbulu, a shop in town, and three Land Cruisers that took passengers and goods between Mbulu and Arusha daily.

He was only alert in meetings if there was anything to

discuss about money, and we would regularly drop coins on the desk, which had the effect of instantly stirring him from a bored torpor when discussion strayed from finances. He spent much of his time on his mobile phone, keeping close tabs on his employees, particularly the drivers. On our tour of church areas, in my first year as Head of the Department of Evangelism, I had taken him along to help encourage giving and accountability from our members. I remember thinking that the village cockerels were being erratic and crowing at times other than dawn, until I realised it was the ringtone on his very active phone.

Andy Martin, from MAF Scotland, came out for a month on two separate occasions. He accompanied me on my scheduled safaris around our rural areas and added some fresh teaching. I translated his messages as best I could, though my Swahili didn't do their complexity justice. I learned to ask him for an overview and identified problem terminology in advance. We laughed!

On one occasion in Singida we had a very busy schedule. We were staying at the farmhouse of Daniel Ng'ene, the Area Leader. Andy had, on arrival in Dar, been bitten once by a mosquito. He didn't mention it, but in Singida he started complaining of feeling ill. His moans and groans were audible through the thin mud wall between his room and ours. Ruth and I rolled our eyes, thinking, 'Men!'

For a couple of days, we left early in the morning and came back around 10pm, having covered our own and Andy's teaching/discussion slots, shown endless films after dark, and done everything necessary to honour the promises made to our village brothers and sisters. One night, when we got home, Andy seemed worse, so despite the risks of driving through the bush at night, off we set. I drove fast despite the rough road and we arrived at the big rural hospital gate, where the guard let us in. Andy, meanwhile, had spent most of the trip unconscious, and the first thing he was aware of was a blinding white light and a silhouetted figure with its arms outstretched. It took him a moment to realise that the figure was not Jesus welcoming him to Heaven, but an orderly carrying him into the hospital.

The doctor we eventually saw was drunk, but he managed to confirm that Andy's vital signs were okay. He wanted to keep him in, but I politely declined. After all, Andy wasn't suffering from anything more than off-the-scale malaria, dysentery, and tsetse fly sickness!

We found ourselves at 2am on the road back to Singida. We needed Andy to get the right treatment, the diesel was getting low and there was none available on the last visit to the area, and I desperately wanted a cup of tea. Daniel took us to a tiny private dispensary which miraculously was open, staffed, and had the tsetse and the anti-malaria medication Andy needed on site. One small pill and Andy was sitting up, transformed. Not only that, but there was diesel at the petrol station. A kiosk at the bus station was able to provide that longed-for cup of tea, and another the one type of soda that Andy could stomach! My heart and soul were full of praise to God.

When we stopped off at HQ in Babati we left the slowly recovering Andy with Ben and Kelli Shular, whose legendary hospitality sustained many a weary traveller as we continued our trip. We picked Andy up two weeks later on our homeward journey. His health was much improved, although to this day he still dredges up, albeit highly humorously, my and Ruth's apparent lack of concern for his near-death experience.

On one of our trips Ruth and I set off for Thawi, a village well off the beaten track in the heavily Muslim Kondoa region a few hours north of Dodoma. The pastor who'd invited us had been somewhat untruthful. We had agreed that Ruth and I would do our seminar and film ministry Friday to Sunday and that we would give the Gospel Crew (formerly Sifuni Band) a lift with us to do an outdoor evangelistic meeting from Monday onwards. However, all the pastor really wanted was transport for the band, and he had promised them that I would take them back to Dodoma despite having been clearly told that Ruth and I would be going on from Thawi to another location.

As it happened only one of the band turned up, so we had a frantic hour or so travelling around Dodoma trying to find a reasonably priced DVD/CD player so he could at least play the band's CD's using our equipment. The pastor was very glad to have us there despite the stern word I had with him about honesty. He had killed a goat to feed us – at least that's what I thought, but in the end, we got mostly guts and a very small amount of meat in a stew so fatty that the grease congealed on our gums. I thought I had gum disease until I brushed my teeth. We ended up having to sing along with the CDs as if we were the Gospel Crew for the afternoon meetings. I showed 'The Passion of the Christ' film to a fair-size group of Muslim men from the village, and several other Christian films. Many people were drunk all day, but they were very peaceful folks. Lots of people wanted to talk about the Gospel and about 20 said the 'Sinners' prayer'.

We spent a night in Arusha, where it rained so hard that some of the stuff we left in the Land Rover got soaked, so we were drying out booklets, tracts etc. for days afterward. An hour or so north is the Kenyan border, straddled by the town of Namanga. Our little church there had been abandoned by their pastor a year earlier, so we went to encourage them and do some Bible teaching. They were keen students. The guard of the guest house we stayed in was a traditionally dressed Maasai warrior. It seemed incongruous that he spent most of his time ironing other people's clothes. The toilet in the house where they had church I went to only once! It was the worst I had ever been in and that's saying a lot; one minute in there and your skin and clothes stank for hours.

I spent a week in the Meru area with the five small churches we had there. The Meru follow many Maasai traditions. It seemed that all denominations had trouble there and aggravated church splits were normal. When I asked some local Christians why this might be, they told me that, many years ago, the first missionaries to this tribe were cruelly martyred by one circumcision group who proudly claimed that they were protecting their Meru traditions. The two men had their private parts cut off and were mercilessly beaten and tortured as they slowly bled to death.

Subsequent missions were aimed at other tribes and the nearby Chaga chief received the Gospel willingly. To this day the Chaga are well known for being blessed in their businesses, but the Meru not. More recently the Meru Lutheran Church members resorted to house burning, beatings and killings as a protest over not having a Meru bishop. Several years ago, the Lutheran leaders repented for the actions of their ancestors and the chain around the martyrs' graves was removed symbolically to free the tribe from the curse. Our small churches had had many troubles, and we were received well as representatives of the General Assembly to tell them about the vision and direction of the church, and to help them understand basic theology. Boniface, a KLM evangelist, and I also took quite some time to talk to two men who had caused a lot of trouble in the church. Sadly, not much seemed to be achieved. These men were educated at Bible college and felt they were above all authority. But at least we tried; and we had a wonderful time with the church there. I was also able to lead the first Lord's Supper since I was ordained.

I drove into the bush with Boniface to show films at a Maasai boma, the Land Rover gradually filling up with warriors who preferred a lift to walking. During the film show it seemed that everybody was spitting noisily and frequently and there was dung everywhere. My shoes and the wire from the equipment to the generator got covered, and so did I when I was winding it onto the reel. As there was nothing to wash my hands with afterwards, the steering wheel also got covered. But they were very happy indeed – and I got my much anticipated cup of milky tea.

The following day the Area Leader asked us to go and minister in Sunya, a village a long way away, not geographically, but timewise. It took five hours to cover the 90 or so kilometres down a road so bad that we had to stop frequently to assess whether or not the Land Rover would make it. It did! At one point, we lost our way and ended up in a ghost town. Those carrying out illegal farming in this conservation area had recently been evicted violently by government troops and the shells of houses were very obvious. We tried to ask individuals, who had returned in defiance of the law to harvest their maize, for directions, but as soon as we slowed the Land Rover and hailed them they ran off, probably suspecting that we were there to enforce the eviction.

We came across a crowd drinking local beer and they surrounded the vehicle. We told them we were pastors and had lost our way. Their response was that if we had been 'other people' (i.e. troops or spies) only the Land Rover would have remained! They were prepared with machetes, spears, stones, etc. to defend themselves and it was a very remote place. I was very thankful that they had asked before acting, and for the great peace God had placed in our hearts that helped us to talk to them calmly.

Life in Africa is less sanitised than in the West; for example, if you want meat you have to brave the blood and flies and stench of the market. Untreated sickness of people and animals is rife, and on my extensive travels in villages I have had to deal with many sights (and smells) that in truth I would prefer not to have encountered. When someone dies there is no mortuary service to lay out the corpse nicely; it has to be done by friends and family. The five-year-old daughter of a pastor friend of mine was murdered quite deliberately by her uncle, who hit her twice on the head with a heavy wooden 'mche' (used for pounding maize into flour). We had to go the following day to pick up the body from a nearby hospital where it had been taken for the police investigation. I had not intended to help out with the preparations, but the group of ladies who had come for that purpose could not stop the blood from oozing out of Hannah's crushed head, so they asked for help. In Tanzania people expect to see the body just before burial so it was important that the shroud should not be blood-stained.

I went to the dispensary and bought a roll of sticky bandage which we used to tape a plastic bag round the back of her head and ears, leaving her face open to view. The shroud was positioned to hide the bag and tape and we managed to put her face almost straight. Thankfully, in the coffin in the dim light of the room, Hannah looked almost as she had done in life. Her parents, who had no other children, still had to deal with the dreadful pain and difficult questions, but their faith in God was strong despite it all and that pulled them through. Whether one lives in the first world or the third, there are no easy answers to pain and suffering.

CHAPTER 16

A TRIP TO GELAI

The most memorable trip to Gelai was the final one. I will describe it in full as it well illustrates the sort of challenges that we encountered on most of our safaris.

It was still the rainy season, so the flat plains were muddy and had to be negotiated with care, and in some cases it was necessary to build up speed to get over the sticky mud patches that a heavy Land Rover would sink into. Makarote, a young and unpopular pastor, met us at the main road and we set off; a giraffe in the road, a herd of eland grazing under a stand of trees, ostrich racing off to the side, and signs of elephant (fresh dung and broken tree branches on the road sides) made it a fun journey. Our tyre tracks were clearly left along the way. Arriving at Gelai, we were welcomed by a group from the two churches at the old mission house.

We settled into the relative luxury of the western furnishings and bath house with hot water from a log burner. We then drove to the village to have lunch in Daniel Minututayu's town house and set up and tested our equipment for the evening's film show. This we did completely unaware that the game wardens, seeing our tracks and a white Land Rover, thought we were poachers and were spying on us from among the crowd gathering for the film show. They only left, persuaded that we weren't poachers, after the start of the show.

As illustrated by my run-in with the pig in Chad, my digestive system often became lazy and was only persuaded to function by the use of the Senokot pills I brought from the UK. I didn't know that this isn't the best way to deal with such things. Being away from home for often over four weeks at a time meant I had to do something. Since arriving in Gelai I had taken pills, done sit-ups and pushed too hard, solving the immediate problem but causing that most painful of conditions.

During lunch I was able to sit on the padded sofa, but in the evening, standing under a tree during the film show, things felt a bit cool in the breeze, and putting my hand down I discovered the seat of my smart skirt soaking wet. The haemorrhoids were leaking profusely, so at the evening meal I sat in Daniel's plastic chair to avoid messing his sofa. Thankfully, he was out during the meal and so I was free to do so. I was able to control the situation using sanitary towels that I had brought along for the usual purposes and was thankful for the soap, hot water and evening breezes available at our HQ to restore my skirt to pristine condition.

During dinner, we had the radio on and heard an official announcement about Rift Valley Fever, an incurable disease which causes one to internally bleed to death. Movement of goats and cattle from affected areas were prohibited and milk and meat had to be cooked for at least 75 minutes to be safe. One of the areas mentioned in the list was Gelai. Maasai are renowned for eating raw meat and serving it rare to visitors, often with the partly roasted lumps of flesh sitting in a pool of bloody fluid on the plate. Neither would the milky tea that we would be given be boiled for 75-plus minutes.

It was good that Daniel was out as it gave us time to discuss and pray about what to do. How could we turn down generously offered food when we still had a whole week to be with them? There was no other place nearby that we could reasonably find provisions, even supposing we decided to be culturally rude. So, we committed ourselves to the God we were there to serve, found access to that peace from Him that doesn't depend on circumstances, and ate the most cooked bits of meat on the plate brought to us with thanks in our hearts.

Films over, we packed up in the dark night and retired to our HQ, where I was able to get myself cleaned up and organised to deal with the current health issue. Naturally, I was accosted in the dark by an enthusiastic dog, who was off his tether after dark, on every trip between the main house and the toilet. I couldn't sleep because of the pain, so I found the requisite medical book that missionaries have. It informed me that it would take five days for the condition to heal itself, and there was no dispensary nearby to get any medication. It was tempting to consider staying in bed and cancelling all activities that required my presence, but I thought to myself, 'I did not come all this way to lie in bed feeling sorry for myself. I will get up, get dressed and behave normally, and do everything we planned for this week! Help me, Lord!'

The next day we were scheduled to drive up a road that would be impassable if it rained at all, to the next village where there was a KLM church. On my last visit we had walked, with me in my smart impractical shoes, which was tough but achievable. This time, getting in and out of the Land Rover was excruciating and the driver's seat seemed designed to put pressure on my most sensitive area. The bumps in the road didn't help either!

However, we got there and had tea in a farmstead which was built of cow dung on a big patch of more cow dung. We copied the residents, keeping our hands over our mugs to stop flies drowning in our tea. When I needed to relieve myself, I walked around the area looking for a sheltered spot. I found one in long damp grass under some low bushes, so I had a job sitting down to complete the painful act whilst looking out for scorpions and poisonous snakes and trying to keep off the small black biting flies that accosted every inch of damp skin they could find. Thankfully it all worked.

Afterward I noticed that my shoes seemed to have stained

my toes because of the damp grass – so I thought! It turned out later that I had maggots in my toe which, when removed, left quite an impressive hole! However, I remembered something valuable; because I'd had a persistent gum infection, I had a store of effective pain medication. I found two of the pills in the Land Rover, and with just one, all pain was history. The relief cannot be expressed by mere words. My thankful spirit soared. Sometimes you must go through pain in order to fully appreciate the cure!

On our trip to the upper village I left my assistants Daudi and Msufa to show the films. I was very weary from the few days with my painful complaint, so went to lie down on my camp bed in the cow dung hut. At one point, I decided to go and see how things were going, and found that I had been locked in and nobody could hear my cries above the noise of the video. After a long time of making as much noise as possible, a passer-by heard and got someone to let me out.

At one film showing a lady came forward for prayer making dreadful growling noises. She had an evil spirit which identified itself as a Bush Lion (and certainly her face was contorted to resemble a growling lion) which, it said, had killed four of her children. It wouldn't leave, although it denied having a right to be there and at one point it told her not to tell us everything. Eventually we found out that, when she went to the witch doctor, he had given her a number of taboos to obey and she had been doing so ever since, giving the spirit a hold on her. During the week, she started recalling more of the taboos. My position is that an evil spirit should never be given a platform to speak while we are presenting the Gospel, and casting them out should never be a sideshow or distraction, so I took her aside to pray with her in private, and the evil spirit left her.

In the West, many Christians have never encountered evil spirits, and may doubt that they are still active in people, or confuse them for mental illness or epilepsy. Though I had not been inhabited by evil spirits in my wild days, I had been aware of their threatening presence, so there was never a question for me that they were real and active, and I had read up on how to deal with them. One encountered them from time to time in the bush culture rife with witchcraft. Ruth Kambenga was enormously helpful in understanding this dark side of African culture and how to discern evil spirits.

Mental illness is not in any way similar to demon possession. When an evil spirit is confronted with the Name of Jesus, it will become agitated, possibly aggressive, and the person will try to avoid eye contact. It is important to force the person to make and keep eye contact with you, and then to ask their name. The demon will reply, often in a strange or distorted voice. You must then pray and command the spirit to depart in Jesus' Name; if there are multiple spirits, you must first bind them so that they all come out at once. Sometimes you have to command them several times before they finally obey, and all the time you are praying, you should keep your eyes open, as the spirit will take any opportunity to lash out at you. When the spirit departs, the person may cough or vomit or have a seizure, or there may be no dramatic reaction at all.

You know the demon is gone when the person is able to tell you their real name, in their real voice. Most importantly of all, you must then pray with them, helping them to ask Jesus to come and inhabit their heart; for as He taught, if that space is left empty the demons will return and bring others worse than themselves. You can only cast out evil spirits where their host is willing and wanting to be free of them. Otherwise they will not allow you to intercede for them. After the demon departs, both the cleansed person and the person praying for them feels very emotionally drained.

In the early hours of our last night in the top village, I awoke to the muffled sound of raindrops on the grass and mud roof of the hut. Sleep was instantly banished as I prayerfully considered how we were going to get out the next morning. The road was impassable after rainfall, but we had the next part of our safari to move on to and many people waiting for us. Because of the weakness of the mobile phone reception in village locations, I had put together the entire year's schedule with the Area Leaders when we met at the Annual General Assembly in Babati in the previous November. The chance of contacting the next area we were scheduled to visit was small. What were we to do? The full responsibility for making the decision fell to me as the driver. People's lives were in my hands. The usual response of nationals to any discussion of risks was, 'No problem, let's just go, God will protect us!' I could only conclude that, being non-drivers, they really didn't understand the difficulty of the driving conditions, risk to the integrity of the vehicle, potential cost of rescue or repairs, and danger to human life and limb. I had to weigh up all the factors prayerfully and make the best decision I could.

The next morning, over milky tea, they gave me their usual automatic approval. I decided to try the road. The first part involved driving on the slippery mud tops of previously created deep ruts, trying to avoid sliding off, taking the sump out, or getting stuck. This done, we moved on to a slippery grass surface and the four men got out, leaving me alone with a Maasai *Coco* (old lady) as they surveyed the track ahead to guide me through. To avoid a deep gully that the rain had gouged out on the trackside, I drove over what looked like a safe bare, rocky surface. The rock, it transpired, was only a big stone. It shifted, and Matilda tilted at a dangerous angle. Daudi, who was closest, looked alarmed. I sat there wanting to get out, but knowing if I did the shift in weight might topple Matilda, and there wasn't another vehicle within hours to rescue us if she did. I did my usual internal focusing on God, asking Him if we were at risk or safe. I felt that deep peace that comes only from Him wiping away the superficial emotional rollercoaster, and I was able to calmly follow Daudi's directions to get off the stone and safely onto firmer ground – three heart-stopping reverses and forward manoeuvres.

Daudi remembered a story he had heard about two men sent out on a rough sea in a small boat to rescue some people in another boat in distress. One of the men asked the other, 'How are we going to get back to safety?'

'We were sent out to rescue those in peril, not to think about how to get back safely.' This we subsequently adopted as our Department's ethos; not to be obsessed with our own comforts or concerns but to put others first at all times, whatever the cost to ourselves.

The next and longest part of the descent was over a deep mud track with large stones embedded and invisible, a potential danger to the undercarriage. However, with my constant prayers for skill and protection and the chaps' diligence, we got down safely and retired to the comfort of the old mission base. I was not in pain anymore and Matilda was still in good shape.

Next stop was Magugu via Babati, where I removed the maggots from my toes. Yona Saki, the Area Leader, had heard of a church plant in a village some distance from his place but within his area and he wanted to visit. In the absence of public transport, what I could offer was my driving skills, Matilda, and our film equipment if wanted. We spent the night at his relatively nice home – bricks and bati (corrugated iron sheet roofing) – and enjoyed good food cooked by his wife, a nurse.

Next day we set off and travelled quite a distance along a 'shortcut' through a wooded area where it was clear that vehicles had not passed for a long time. There were huge puddles in deep, steep dips in the track, and Yona's skill in assessing how and where best to cross was the only way we got through. We found the pastor conducting the funeral of a young child at a farmstead and living in a very primitive hut in the woods, and we met his congregation. This tribe were cattle herders and turned up for meetings at 2pm regardless of whatever agreement had previously been made as this was the time they had finished tending their livestock and were free. They never seemed to settle but continuously talked amongst themselves and moved around. The women, half naked, swapped naked toddlers and babies from one breast to another.

The KLM pastor had had great trouble from pastors of other denominations spreading rumours that he had been lying about the denomination and that it didn't exist, as no leader had visited. Four bona fide leaders turning up at a well-attended funeral must have gone a fair way toward refuting these claims, which had led to half the church leaving. Boniface preached well despite the restless chickens, goats and dogs that wandered around amongst the crowds sitting on the dusty earth, and the little body (the parents' fourth child to die) was duly buried beside the house in a shroud under a covering of banana leaves and sticks and then soil.

As Yona's letter to the pastor hadn't arrived, he hadn't made arrangements for us, so we headed for the nearest village to find food, buying a couple of live chickens en route. The track through the forest had been cleared for bicycles and had tyre-piercing fine stumps all over it. Thankfully I managed to avoid them and we arrived without incident. It is essential to report to the church chairman's office in every village to introduce oneself and explain one's presence – this would normally have been done in advance by our pastor, but of course, unaware of our impending arrival, he had not been able. This done, we found a place to eat, and with the chairman's permission, set up the film equipment. However, the rigours of our journey had caused a technical problem that affected the sound and we had to quit.

We met with the church and introduced ourselves as from HQ and explained the KLM setup and Yona was able to plan future visits. At the end of our two-day visit we went off to track down another church plant to do the same again, this time at a teacher's residence in a nearby village down the stumpy track, and then the rollercoaster-and-puddle section of the shortcut to the main road.

Msufa's wife and I had been offered a bed in the hut of a

church elder's wife, perhaps the most beautiful woman I have ever seen, and the guys were to sleep in the pastor's hut. The bed we shared was a wooden frame with string and covered by a cowhide. I got out the sleeping bags and was settling down for the night when the lady of the house remarked, 'Oh, I forgot to say, we are terribly bothered by bedbugs!'

This was accurate.

It was a night of fitful sleep punctuated by wakefulness to sweep the bugs off our faces, limbs and bodies. But they are notorious for coming straight back and even following if you move outside and a distance away from an infested hut. It was a great relief to soothe the itchy red lines of bites in a bucket of hot water the next morning. However, the bugs were in all of our belongings, continuing their predations ceaselessly. One could feel them crawling over one's skin but couldn't kill them as they had moved on before your hand got to where they had just bitten.

On return to our village base I bought a can of fly spray and hung all of my clothes on the washing line in bright sunlight and sprayed them. Small things were put in my bag, the zip almost closed, and spray used copiously inside before sealing the bag for hours. It took days before the bugs were eradicated. Meanwhile, I smelled like fly spray and was glad that Sunday's service was in a breezy woodland clearing and not an enclosed space. After the service, we were invited to bless a Maasai homestead. Again, the Rift Valley Fever issue was raised, and the barely cooked goat meat came out sitting in a pool of red blood. Again, silent but fervent prayer went up – to eat or not to eat? The peace of God swept aside the usual emotional turmoil and I ate with confidence, choosing the most cooked-looking bits. The elder men cut uncooked bones with their pangas (machetes) to get the marrow.

We were then invited to visit the individual huts on the boma. It was interesting to see how different the huts of the Maasai are to the Gogo huts, with Y-shaped trunks supporting the logs of the bases but, as all are cattle herders, the smell of milk and the charcoal used to sterilise milk gourds and cured cow-skin were similar. To me, it was a smell of home – but not for much longer.

CHAPTER 17

IN GOD'S OWN COUNTRY AGAIN

For my last few years in Tanzania I knew that my ageing parents needed an annual visit. So every December, our church's quiet month, I flew home just to see how they were doing. In December 2007 I was leafing through one of Dad's science magazines and saw a job that I knew I could do. The words came into my mind, 'and when the time comes I will have the right job for you!'

I was surprised! When I had decided to follow the call of God to Africa, I had counted the cost up to the point of spending the rest of my life and dying there. The high turnover at MAF Dodoma just confirmed me in my conviction that I didn't want to return to my somewhat nomadic earlier life, and planned instead to stay put for as long as possible. I had put a great deal of effort into assimilating into the culture and learning the language, and I had just completed the refurbishment of the houses I had bought two years earlier. Returning to the UK wasn't in my thinking. However, on my arrival back in Tanzania something had changed. That feeling of being 'in the right place' had gone, replaced with recurring thoughts like 'This might be the last time I drive down this road or see this person or....' There is, after all, a last time for everything. I had to extract my fingers from a great many pies, while taking care not to get involved in anything new.

In the meantime, the monthly safaris to our remote village churches went on relentlessly. I arranged (and paid for) a three-day convention for all of our pastors. One of the attractions was Pastor Abihudi Mishole singing his wonderful anti-poverty-mentality songs. As happens even in the UK, people born into and long accustomed to poverty become stuck in the attitude that nothing will ever change and that there are no options in their lives and, with this mindset, they can become defeatist and self-pitying. Not all needy people are interested in bettering their lot through hard work and wise use of resources, and this applies to projects as well as to individual cases. Songs like the ones sung by Pastor Mishole or the Sifuni Band taught people that hard work and trust in God means that they are free to take control of their lives and work their way out of poverty. Becoming a Christian doesn't guarantee a prosperous life, but it grants contentment even in the midst of hardship.

The General Assembly was scheduled for November, and I booked my flights for the end of month so that I could say my farewells. However, for some reason the Assembly was delayed, so I wrote a letter and gave it to Dismus to read out. It saved much trouble for me. Leaving Tanzania was like leaving Sammy; excruciating, but the right thing for the time.

It is always tempting, having left the mission field, for ex-missionaries to hold on to their previous life by supporting their favourite nationals financially, giving advice and generally interfering. It became clear over the years working in Tanzania that many of the current problems in the national church were caused by ex-missionaries, and so I made a decision, 'When you're gone, you're gone!' If one wanted to send finances, it could be done only through recognised projects, supported through official and accountable channels.

There was one missionary who had been sending money for decades to support seven OAP's. The money was sent directly to a very corrupt man whom they trusted from their time on the field, and they assumed he was using the money as arranged.

When it was discovered that something might not be quite right and enquiries were made, it turned out that there were no OAP's being supported and the money was unaccounted for. He had used it as his own allowance, enabling him to be more influential in life than he could have achieved by himself. In fact, further investigation showed that he had been able to pull rank and steal tractors and other equipment that had been bought for the community. This was not uncommon so I made sure I had closure before I left, and have adopted a policy of no contact with any of my former colleagues. Even a phone call could lead to being manipulated into doing something harmful. It was a tough decision when we had been through so much together, and a huge loss.

The last few weeks in Tanzania I wrestled with some of the consequences of moving back to the UK. What job could I possibly do? In Africa I had become so honed for missionary life – I was like a polished arrow shot from a bow for a specific target. It left me a jack of many trades, but very inferior by Western standards, where everyone seemed to have a small but very specific field of true expertise. I went online and found a great job in Alaska maintaining a Cessna 206 used for tourism during the four summer months, but I knew that I couldn't apply. God was asking me to return to Scotland.

At 45 I didn't want to live with Mum and Dad. I remembered the generosity of Ruth Box from MAF and the peaceful times I had spent at her home each time I came to the UK on Home Assignment. I said to the Lord that I would like to stay with her, but I wouldn't ask her – I would wait to see if it was His provision. A few days later Andy Martin was in Tanzania and passed a verbal message from Ruth herself saying that she had heard I was moving back and was welcome to stay with her until I got myself sorted! Another tangible answered prayer, and one showing that the move to Scotland was right. Then there was the question, again, of my much-loved dogs. What was His plan for them? I was considering giving the houses away at the time; however, I became increasingly convinced that this was not the way forward and soon I had a lovely couple lined up to live rent-free in the house as long as they looked after the dogs, cat, workers and the property (in that order of importance, based on levels of vulnerability).

I gradually handed over my responsibilities to my assistant Daudi Garang, gave Matilda and the film equipment to the Department of Evangelism, left a year's budget for running the Department, gave the household over to my new lodgers, and finally left. As my friend Katja was also leaving Tanzania permanently to return to Germany, as a treat we joined a day trip on an MAF plane to Ruaha Game Park.

It was glorious! We got so close to calm grazing elephants in a wood that every pore and hair on their faces was visible and one could look in their eyes and they looked back. It felt risky being so close, but it was memorable. A pride of 19 lions lounged lazily, having recently fed. The stink was almost unbearable as we were downwind, and the hordes of flies clinging to urine-soaked areas of their coats made one cringe. How uncomfortable could that be! We had lunch at the lodge and I spoke to the lady running it. I knew the Foxes, who owned the lodge, because MAF had sold them several of our old C206's and we performed routine maintenance for them.

Katja and I also travelled to Dar together on our final outbound journey and had fun at a craft fair, looking at lovely artefacts and buying Tinga Tinga art from the market. A trip in a Dar tuk-tuk was cheap and allowed travel round side streets and a chance to be exposed to the inevitable interesting smells. We had chai and chapattis in a locals' cafe. That caramelized taste of the tea, milk and sugar boiled for hours is my favourite. And in the warm evening we had a high-class meal in a seaside seafood restaurant, basking in the damp air. It was a good way to say goodbye, until I arrived at the airport and was informed that two days earlier BA had changed their baggage regulations. Whereas previously they would accept two bags at 31kg, it was now 23kg per bag. I had to open my bags and jettison as much as possible, giving my clothes to the airport staff. Sadly, it meant that, in my haste, I didn't pack my big Tinga Tinga painting as well as possible, and to this day in a certain light the damage is visible. It is a good reminder not to be materialistic. Hold one's possessions lightly, travel light and, as good old Scottish R.L. Stevenson said, 'travel hopefully'.

MAF gave me a modest lump sum to help with starting up again. Dad generously gave me his old car and bought a nice new one and I moved in with Ruth Box up in Kirkintilloch. For eleven months, I was unemployed. I applied for jobs, went on a course to update my CV, did the housekeeping as thanks for staying rent-free in this busy, selfless lady's peaceful home, and attended two suicide intervention courses and a mental health first aid course. My parents pressured me to get a job. I was supposed to be resting, but as I said to God, 'It isn't easy to rest when you don't know how long it's going to take to get a job!' Ruth McKelvey called me and said, 'God will give you a chance to get yourself settled – then the rubber will hit the road and you'll know why He told you to come back.' Job applications were rejected or went unanswered. Any replies were ungracious and unhelpful.

Then I got a phone call from Tanzania. Bracken, my beloved watchdog, had attacked my tenant and torn the skin on her jaw. She was traumatised. The best I could do for him was to insist that he be shot rather than calling a vet to have him injected, so he would have a more peaceful death than Caroline's poor dog Lady. He was shot on Valentine's Day 2010. My heart was sore and tears were many.

Carol McCusker, who had given me a home before my travelling to Tanzania, had gone off to Spain and then come back to the UK. On one of my Home Assignments she had told me she'd found the most wonderful job counselling people with debt problems via a ministry called Christians Against Poverty (CAP). When I heard the details of CAP's setup by the remarkable, generous John Kirkby and how it all worked, it blew me away. I thought, 'If I ever come back to the UK and have wealth I will support this!'

Amazingly, on my return to Scotland I saw a vacancy advert online for a CAP Centre Manager for Holy Trinity Church of Scotland (HTC), Wester Hailes. They only ever recruit in-house at the local church, which set up the Centre. I called Carol and asked if she thought I should apply. She said that if ever there was a job tailor-made for me, this was it!

I got an interview for the job and was accepted. God's promise of the right job for me had come true. However, the CAP job was in Edinburgh and I needed a place to stay. Mike and Evelyn Banks generously agreed to share their lovely home in Kirkliston. I went to the CAP prayer meeting there to meet them. I said 'Lord, if this is the right place for me, let there be a dog.' And behold, Rosie Woo, the adorable Cavalier King Charles, was there in all her glory. We became firm friends.

For seven months I lived with them, at first going back and forth to Ruth's, and then full-time. House hunting was tough, but one day Evelyn said to me, 'Don't worry, God has the right house for you just round the corner!' A few days later she texted me at work to let me know that the house on the corner opposite their home had just gone on the market. I was able to buy it with no mortgage and to furnish it with all new things. It was as if God had returned me to the state in life that I would have enjoyed had I chosen a good UK career. He is no man's debtor.

At Mike and Evelyn's, I had lived essentially in one room, with my worldly possessions stacked around me. Much as I loved living with them, my own home sounded like a luxury – but when I moved, I was surprised by how lonely I was. In Africa I'd been used to being surrounded by people, and was constantly needed. Now the space around me felt empty. My good friend Angie, who was the office manager for Holy Trinity and had so warmly invited me for my first CAP job interview, moved in a few houses away. She was a godsend. We were both alone; me single, her a widow. There was no support group for singles in our church, so we became each other's support group. I was used to popping in and out of people's houses without any need for strict scheduling, and often one of us would show up at the other's door in her pyjamas, in need of an impromptu prayer meeting! We often met to pray on a Friday, and every New Year we would get together to seek the Lord's plans for us over the coming year.

The CAP Centre Manager's job was wonderful and a huge challenge. I needed help, and one of the first people to come along was Margaret. She was a wonderful befriender, and despite her obvious abilities didn't have employment, so she gave of her time very generously. One day she came into the office and said she felt God asking her to support me. I was holding my own in most areas of the job except the monthly financial stuff. So dear Margaret, who was already running the café and senior citizen group accounts, took on the CAP accounts too. Then the church decided they needed an admin person, and Margaret was the obvious choice. She really needed more hours for it to be good employment, and I would often tell her that she could easily do the whole CAP job. She would demur, but I knew she had all the qualities needed.

I'd already come across many people stuck in a poverty mentality in Tanzania. The causes and living standards involved might be different, but people everywhere are the same. What the impoverished Scots I encountered through CAP needed was someone with the art of listening without interruption, judgement, inattention or impatience. Good listening made people who often felt useless and hopeless see that they had value, that their stories did matter. It was of great importance not to pre-judge anyone or make assumptions about why they were in debt, because each story was unique and sometimes it wasn't the person's fault. Even when they had fallen into debt through bad choices, the most effective way to give them hope was to make them feel accepted as they were – just as I had been accepted in Christ while I was in life's pits. In this way, they could see that debt didn't have to control or define them, and we were always upfront in offering Christ as the solution to life's problems.

This could be demanding work – I often went to see clients who were in a bad way outside business hours – but in Africa I had been surrounded by need all the time, and had built up a high tolerance to it. In comparison, I felt I was simply giving a reasonable amount of care. I was also used to helping people set and stick to budgets, which was really the main focus of CAP's work.

One thing I did not do was allow myself to feel over-burdened by people's decisions. There were a number of times that I sensed people were close to suicide, and I felt the best way to deal with this was straight talk, not a lingering discussion. 'Are there tablets I need to take from you?' As far as I know, none of the clients considering suicide ever went through with it, but I knew that God, and not I, was responsible for life and death and people's eternal souls. In the same way that I commended Aunt Nan to the Lord, as I couldn't know the final state of her soul, so I laid my burdens for my family, friends and clients on His shoulders.

One client, Angela, had been suffering from depression after losing both parents, and her way of coping was retail therapy. She went off work, couldn't pay her bills, and her debt got out of control. Her husband Iain brought her to CAP in October 2009, they gained control of their finances and in March 2010 Angela became a Christian. She spoke at 'Discovery', an 'Inspire' conference in Edinburgh, CAP Sunday at the church and 'CLAN' (Christian Living Across the Nation). She decided she wanted to be baptised and asked me to be her godmother, witnessing her public profession that she was a daughter of Christ. She bought me a beautiful silver cross necklace as a thank you gift, which I treasured, but not more than seeing how her life had changed. Angela even held a fundraiser ceilidh (This simply means 'meeting' in Gaelic, but usually entails exuberant dancing to folk music!) for CAP and ended up joining them as a support worker – from client to colleague in just a few years! And this arc was by no means unusual.

So, work was full of encouragements, but in the midst of it all I found myself struggling to fully adapt to UK life. Africa is a tough place to live in many ways, but it also has so much to enjoy. The UK, in contrast, can be relatively easy and it was a relief not to be pointed out or stared at in public as the only white face in the vicinity – but there are things that I found unexpectedly hard. One example would be the NHS, which I found unbearably legalistic. In Africa one had to take a lot of responsibility for health. I was careful and proactive. If bitten by ticks, a short course of the right meds was available for a very small cost from a local pharmacy in Dodoma. But back in the UK, even for something relatively minor by comparison, one had to take time off work for a medical appointment, waste the medic or dentist's time to get a prescription which has to go through the pharmacy at a cost, and comes in packaging that has to be recycled. What a waste!

So many things struck me as bizarre in Scotland; the array of luxuries from perfumes to Christmas decorations, the fact that a haircut cost the equivalent of a month's wages for a Tanzanian engineer, the baffling assortment of kettles and washing machines for sale. I was utterly grateful when an HTC friend, Sue, offered to go with me to choose a settee. I felt overwhelmed in the store and her presence kept me grounded. In Dodoma I would have had virtually no choice, very likely buying a used one from a resident who was moving on, or I may well have had to get one built from scratch, as I did with my bed frame when I moved off the MAF compound.

Two years after returning to the UK, I got a useful and, as ever, timely call from Ruth McKelvey, seemingly out of the blue. She told me that, according to MAF research, this would be the time when Reverse Culture Shock could well set in. I had not even considered it. Setting up in the UK had taken my attention and energy, and formal debriefing had been minimal. She was so right! I had been feeling really odd emotionally, almost on the brink of a breakdown and with no obvious reason. Her words cut through the fog and just hearing a bit more about RCS set me free.

The fact is that, as a missionary, you ask God to give you His heart for the land and its people and, when He does, you feel corresponding heartbreak when you have to leave them. You think you're coming home, but 'home' now feels foreign. You don't belong anywhere.

If I could combine the best of Africa and UK and get rid of the less good bits out of each, then this world would be closer to Heaven for me. Imagine a country with clean Western toilets, but also African doughnuts! I missed my colleagues and all our laughter, and found it hard to get accustomed to seeing almost entirely white faces again. Living cross-culturally, whilst a rich experience, has its challenging moments – and just as many in the 'civilised' UK as in tribal Africa.

Soon after starting with CAP, I realised I would need another part-time job to boost my income. I saw an advert for an admin post with Dignity Alert and Research Foundation (DARF), which educates and campaigns against Female Genital Mutilation. I applied and, at the interview, I was amazed to find a panel of three Tanzanian women. The interview began in English and finished in Swahili! One of the panel was Dr Monica Magoke-Mhoja, a human rights lawyer and founder of the organisation. I found that I already knew a little about her, because a Glaswegian friend had mentioned to me that we had a great deal in common and a similar love for God – yet another God-incidence!

FGM was a problem in Scotland, but because very little research had been done on it, we didn't know the extent. In Africa one of my housemates had been 'circumcised', and certainly we had dealt with it in the villages, but many Westerners don't appreciate the diversity of the issue and the reasons behind it. For example, in Dodoma it's considered a mark of cleanliness, but some tribes do it to guard against promiscuity. Some very minor tribes do it as a sacrifice to their gods, or believe they'll be cursed if they don't do it. In others, it's seen as a prerequisite for marriage. Yet it can lead to serious bleeding, psychological effects, and even death, particularly where medical attention is unavailable or sub-par.

The job was hard work. I had a lot to learn and the whole office needed ordering but, as always, I am a good sorter-outer and organiser. I made some valuable contacts, and the news about FGM started to spread, albeit slowly.

I recruited a number of volunteers to help out in the office with raising funds and awareness. I had to attend lots of meetings of groups with similar interests. I managed to interest the police, although the first contact I made was almost traumatised by the DVD I showed her as an intro. But it led to being invited to speak at big events.

One day while speaking Swahili with Monica, I noticed that her manner of speaking was very familiar. 'You remind me of my friend in Dodoma,' I told her.

'Who is your friend?' Monica asked.

'Ruth Kambenga; we were ministry partners for many years.'

Monica laughed. 'Ruthie is my niece!'

From then on I called Monica 'Dada' – sister.

Monica, who like me, couldn't sit still when she saw a need to be filled, also decided to start a Swahili service in Edinburgh. She came to speak to me before anyone else, but I was familiar with the difficulties of being a pastor from my KLM days, and I warned Monica about the uphill battle ahead of her. Nevertheless, I told her I'd do anything I could to help, short of joining the committee – that was off the cards.

But of course, being able to worship in a Tanzanian community again was irresistible, and I ended up doing everything from translating to preaching to leading a worship conga line. How could I turn down the opportunity to have a little bit of Africa back? It also gave me an opportunity to make use of Carol, another former

CAP client who had come out of poverty. She liked working the sound desk at Holy Trinity services, so I asked her to man it for the Tanzanian service that took place once a month after the normal HTC service. This required great flexibility, as we might have four people scheduled to sing but would often end up with ten! Carol struggled with self-doubt and hadn't had much encouragement from her family to go to college, but I could see that she had a real knack for her work. There was much rejoicing when she got her National Qualification in sound engineering and then an a Higher National Diploma in sound production.

Like Ruth before her, Monica and her family became my family. One of her daughters had a Scottish boyfriend and wanted to get engaged, but Monica didn't want her to get married too young; however, she wanted to be open to the Lord's leading in the situation. Usually in Tanzanian culture the parents would meet to discuss the young couple's future and, normally, the groom's family would pay a dowry, but being a human rights lawyer, Monica didn't entertain this idea. She wanted nothing but for Jesus to be the centre of her daughter's life.

Seeing that I could interpret culture as well as language, Monica asked me to become the liaison between the two families! Everyone sat down in Monica's living room, and I explained to the groom's family that these were very well-off people at home, God-fearing, and respectable; Monica's dad had been an Anglican priest. They weren't hut-dwellers!

Actually, the biggest discussion point was about the wedding menu. Monica's family were teetotal, but the boy's family were Roman Catholic and liked to raise a glass or two at special occasions. Monica felt it was important not to interfere with either tradition, so in the end there were two parties – a 'dry' lunch after the church ceremony and then a dinner party hosted by the groom! The marriage was at the Registry Office and I went along with the other DARF volunteers, glad for another excuse to get out my African dress.

Around November 2010 I felt that a year at DARF was as much

as I could reasonably do. Two part-time jobs, both of which were busy, were more than one full-time job. We recruited another Programme Officer and I left in December. It was hard work but the results have been amazing, and now FGM is on the map. The new people who have joined have taken the work forward, building on what we achieved. It was worth it!

For almost four years I had had a long-distance bit-more-than-a-friendship with a gentleman. While we had been mostly separated by vast distances, I had exceptionally missed him, prioritised spending time with him on Home Assignment, and considered myself 'off the market'. Returning to the UK and getting a job in Edinburgh where he had his bachelor pad seemed to me to be signs that maybe more would develop. But it didn't, and so through a year of inner turmoil, I gradually came to the point where I couldn't go on. I had done everything I could to show commitment, and it was now obvious that that was not returned. With a heavy, hurting heart I went for a long country walk, and at a point where the instructions were unclear, I asked someone I met for guidance.

The good-looking wheelchair-bound man and I hit it off. He was polite and not pushy. We struck up a friendship – 'A ray of sunshine,' I felt God to say to me. We exchanged numbers and some weeks later met up for a walk. However, although he showed some interest and gave me the courage to formally make the break with my boyfriend, he wasn't the marrying sort. He had a grown daughter and a grandchild who very properly took first place in his life. This was completely understandable, but my prayer partner Angie said, 'You shouldn't be second place to the man in your life. We need to ask God for the very best He has for you.'

It was true that I was lonely, fed up with being single, and wanted my parents to see me settled and provided for. Angie and I wrote and prayed through a list of what I needed in a husband. I wanted someone who would enjoy discussion and stimulating conversation, have a sense of humour, love animals and travel, and quickly connect with my family in Galloway. I particularly wanted to feel that I could enrich this man's life in whatever ways God chose.

It was a week later that I met Neil through work. An alcohol counsellor, he sounded nice on the phone as we arranged to meet. At the risk of sounding like a teenage girl, I have a couple of exclamation marks next to the entry of his name in my diary on 12th October 2010! We instantly liked each other and he was good at sending highly amusing texts every few days. However, I kept a bit of a distance, partly because I was still technically with the man I had met on my walk, but also because our jobs dovetailed. We had to be careful to maintain confidentiality and not share specifics about our work, even though we each found the other's organisation useful for our clients. To be on the safe side, I disclosed our friendship to my line manager – I was very concerned to avoid any conflict of interest. Meanwhile, when Angie and I met to pray – in our pyjamas(!) – I was always telling her more about the wonderful Neil. Everything about him seemed so right for me.

One day I was driving down to Norheim, my parents' home in rural Galloway, in a snowstorm, heading home for Christmas. Neil was sending me very sweet texts, but I could see that he was looking for more than friendship so I pulled over and called him. 'There's a lot in your texts,' I said. 'I just have to tell you that I will not dishonour God, this other man, you, or myself by even considering a relationship until the one I'm in resolves itself.' He very respectfully promised to drop the subject and he kept his word faithfully. It was good to meet such a gentleman, and he seemed somehow different from the other men I'd been interested in over the years.

CHAPTER 18

YET ANOTHER NEW NAME

When I arrived at Norheim for Christmas 2010, after driving through that snowstorm, Dad mentioned that he was struggling to remember some words. After much deliberation, I suggested he get it checked out. He was not keen, but did it anyway. The doctor thought it was probably a minor stroke, gave him some medication and arranged for tests. Soon after getting home he felt really unwell. The doctor told Mum just to drive him to Dumfries hospital as arranged. He was violently sick en route. The tests showed an inoperable tumour in his brain.

We had often talked about what we as a family would do if one of us got cancer, never imagining that we would. He stuck to what he had always said he would do, and refused treatment. The specialist agreed with his decision and gave him four months to live. He wanted to be at home, so we arranged this and the NHS sent a lot of equipment to the house for which we were very grateful in the coming months. To support him and Mum I compressed my CAP work into two days and spent four at Norheim nearly every week. I had left DARF at just the right time.

The car he had given me on my return to the UK needed a major repair, so Dad yet again generously gave me his lovely new car. It could reverse itself into parking spaces, which was a great help in town. Having been used to Matilda the Land Rover and the vast space offered by Africa, my spatial awareness for parking had suffered.

Meanwhile, I was thinking that if I were ever to get married, this was the time. I really wanted Dad to 'give me away'. I put it to my current boyfriend that I was looking for commitment and left him to decide what his intentions were. A week later he gave me his decision; friends only. The last few years had seen some turmoil in my heart, and yet I could see God's hand in both my recent relationships. The first had made me feel feminine and beautiful, not always a common experience for a forty-something who had spent many years in boiler suits. The second had showed me that there were other men out there, and that I could recognise these possibilities despite having felt rejected. Every love in our lives leaves us with valuable lessons and blessings if we are able to receive them instead of focusing on the bitterness and disappointment of their endings.

Four days after my conversation with my now ex-boyfriend, on Valentine's Day 2011, Neil invited me for a coffee. We went for a walk at Bavelaw Castle, an historic house in the city of Edinburgh, and Neil politely asked how things were going with my relationship. It was good to be able to tell him that that question was now resolved. And so we started courting in the bird-hide at Bavelaw. It was wonderful to find someone with an open, loving heart.

Neil was aware that Dad's health was deteriorating, and that I longed for him to see me wed off. Five days after the bird-hide, Neil sent me a text saying, 'If you'll have me, I'm yours.'

I wasn't sure if he was joking or not, and replied, 'Are you serious?'

He sent back, 'Will you marry me?'

I said, 'yes', on one condition – I didn't want a ring, but further down the road, he was to buy me an 'engagement' dog.

It is said 'Marry in haste and repent at leisure,' but we didn't – repent, that is! I had a real confidence in his character that I didn't have in other men. In some ways, I knew he was 'the one' because of the timing, but it was also the kind of person he is. This period was suffused with the feeling of everything falling into place.

At church the following Sunday, Angie encouraged me to ask my pastor, Kenny, when he could marry us. I opened my diary at Saturday 12th March, just over a couple of weeks hence. After the service, I explained the need for haste because of Dad's prognosis, and asked if he could help. The first free day he had was Saturday 12th March.

I went to Norheim and let them know that Neil was coming and why. His mum comes from our neck of the woods, so his family were known to mine. After lunch Mum and I conveniently disappeared on fictional errands and Neil started his well-prepared and, knowing him, very eloquent speech. He didn't get far before Dad said, 'A ken whit yer here fur! Jist get oan wi' it! But mind ye look efter her weel or A'll shoot ye!', forgetting that his guns had been disposed of as soon as he had the cancer diagnosis. The next morning Neil and I went off to the Stranraer Registrar's office and completed the necessary forms with six hours to spare of the two weeks' notice required under Scots law.

Dad wanted the wedding in the North West Castle. I was praying earnestly in my head as it's a popular venue. How could we possibly get it at such short notice? Most people plan weddings at least a year ahead. We arrived, and the page in the diary for the 12th of March was – blank! Phone calls were made to immediate family, all of whom were free, and I went off to a meeting, leaving Neil to make all the wedding decisions with his new in-laws-to-be. They did a splendid job. Flowers, bright, with the best buffet menu and drinks package available, alongside a room in the hotel for our wedding night. All of the female relatives up to my age were invited to be bridesmaids, with instructions to wear something colourful. Neil chose my dress, his favourite out of my Africa collection, complete with spectacular headgear.

The big day arrived soon, but not too soon for us. It was accompanied by all the craziness incumbent on a DIY wedding. I spent some of the morning making a bouquet and then went to the hairdresser's. Dad wanted to cut Mum's hair and was miffed when she said no, but his hands were shaky because of his condition. Then he was irritated by the sleeves on his dress shirt. 'Just wear whatever you want, Dad!' I told him and so he changed to a shirt he liked, and peace was restored.

Mum drove herself to the hotel, and Dad and I followed a few minutes later. He told me off for speeding through Dunragit. I may have broken my speeding habit, but on this particular day I just couldn't wait to arrive. 'It's not a good day for getting stopped for speeding', Dad reminded me. So much for the bride arriving fashionably late – we arrived half an hour early!

The day after the wedding, Neil took his parents home to Edinburgh, and I followed later. Marriage, at our time in life, had to start out with business as usual. Initially we only saw each other for a couple of nights a week as I spent much of my time in Galloway helping Mum and Dad. Neil couldn't move into my house as I had a friend staying. For seven weeks, when I wasn't at Norheim, we stayed wherever we chose; his place or mine. Because the romance had been such a whirlwind, it was good to have time to get to know each other better before making the big move in together.

Two weeks after the wedding we had a short honeymoon in Rome, as we didn't like to leave my parents for too long. Neil had found a flat near the city centre. The owners had a restaurant and gave us a free dinner as a celebration of our recent marriage. We took the bus-top tour and then visited the bits we liked best and we took our first train trip together to a village in the Italian countryside.

Dad was with us for seven months after the diagnosis. Because of my experience with CAP I knew that it's easier to change names on bills and accounts while the person is still able to give permission, so he and I got everything moved into Mum's name. Just after his diagnosis he seemed to have given up. In fact, he stopped eating for days in an attempt to starve himself to death. But with the support of the Macmillan nurse, and a bit of encouragement, he perked up and was able to get up and dressed and did most of the cooking and had visitors. As ever, Mum worked quietly away in the background doing anything that would help him feel he was doing better than he really was. Most days he and I would take a long slow walk, not very far, and talk about many things. We were fully reconciled and at peace with each other, for which I am hugely thankful. I had a great admiration for this sometimes difficult but very great man who had done his best to make the most of every opportunity that he had been presented with in life.

One day he was particularly confused and it was clear that he had had enough. The time had come. The doctor inserted a driver so that drugs could be given intravenously to make him comfortable. For a week, we lived as normally as possible with Dad lying in the sitting room on the special airbed. He passed away peacefully at Norheim in the early afternoon on 2nd August 2011, with Mum by his side and me and Neil close by. As requested, I conducted his funeral at Ayr crematorium, and we buried his ashes with those of my brother Gavin in Kirkinner churchyard in peaceful rural Galloway.

Once I was a little less needed at Norheim, Neil and I had a number of wonderful holidays, including a trip to Tanzania so Neil could have an inkling of my previous life. It was good to be home again. However, as my current tenants were leaving the country, it seemed the opportune time to sell the houses. Emmie had been fired a few months before. I couldn't know what had happened at such a long distance. She was the one who had been there since the beginning and knew everything about the running of the place, and it would have been impractical to keep overseeing the houses from the UK without her. Other than Emmie, Pastor Dismus, and my spiritual twin Ruth, I stuck to my resolution of staying out of my former mission field, and refrained from seeing old friends.

Back home, work became busy again. In addition, Mum was becoming increasingly vulnerable, and two years after Dad passed away, it seemed the right time for her to move closer to me. By the grace of God we got her a beautiful flat in Edinburgh, within walking distance of Sainsbury's and Marks & Spencer. An elder from the local church visited regularly and arranged lifts to church events. And having her only fifteen minutes' drive away was great. However, her memory had been deteriorating noticeably and she lacked her previous confidence, particularly without Dad around. She never really enjoyed the full benefits of such a great place.

For quite some time I'd had a feeling that I would not be in the CAP role for much longer. Angie and I would still get together at the start of every year to ask the Lord what He had in store for us and how we should serve Him, but for the first time in my Christian life, I had only a peaceful silence. Part of married life for me often entailed getting up very early in order to have a couple of hours just in Jesus' company before starting my day with Neil. I would sit and listen to try to discern what God had next for me, but nothing at all came. It reminded me of Rachel in Dodoma, who had died in a car crash many years ago. What I was seeing in front of me was a blank sheet of paper.

CHAPTER 19

THE END OF THE BEGINNING

In March 2013, I found a small lump. It took a couple of weeks to get a doctor's appointment. He immediately put through a referral to the hospital, and I had an appointment the day after Neil and I returned from holiday in the western Mediterranean. The lump was cancerous, but with no sign of cancer spreading to the lymph nodes, it looked like an operation to remove the cancer and some chemo would give me another 20 years. It all seemed quite simple. I would lose weight (my chest deflates on losing weight, so I saw an opportunity to make a virtue out of this necessary surgery), I could get the cancer removed and have a 'boob job' on the NHS and finally have the luxury of being able to buy clothes in ordinary shops for the first time. Taking Mum shopping at M&S, I would eye up possible purchases with anticipation. I thought two or three months off work would be enough. Margaret agreed to fill in for my absence and we set about tackling all the jobs in the office to make the handover easy.

In the midst of all this optimism, a routine X-ray showed something in the lungs. I suggested it might be TB or something I could have contracted in Tanzania. The doctors agreed this was possible. Further ultrasound scans were inconclusive. A biopsy was needed, but there was a significant wait. The outcome was a diagnosis of metastatic breast cancer in the lungs, lymph node and liver, with a five-year life expectancy. The surgery would not now be an option. A tingling in my face a few months later led to more tests, which showed the cancer had spread to my brain. Expectancy was reduced to three months.

The consultant explained the treatment options for the cancer in other areas, all of which sounded unpleasant, and I was glad of having enough time to think over whether it was worth even embarking on the chemo journey. I asked my friend, Evelyn, to come with me to the consultant to pray and help me discern God's guidance. However, in conversation with one of the nurses, she said something that struck me – that if it was God's time for me to go, then there wouldn't be options – and so I chose to try the chemo.

With the steroids I was prescribed to reduce the swelling in my brain, I had a chubby face and, combined with baldness, I resembled the Addams family's Uncle Fester. Neil assured me the look was more Sinead O'Connor. My friend Pam advised me that lipstick helps the appearance when you wear a wig. She was right. So many people said, 'You look so well!'

I do not believe that it is for me to dictate to God, but as His servant, to ask Him what His plans are. I laid the matter before Him and I felt the following come into my thoughts:

1) Do not allow anything to destroy your peace. There is a peace from God, not dependent on circumstances, which guards our hearts and minds (Philippians 4:6-7). But it is a discipline to hold onto it.
2) Do not be distracted – it would be easy to spend all one's time focused on the problem and to miss out on all of the really wonderful things that each day can bring. What a waste of short and precious time.
3) Do not be afraid – this was particularly referring to treatment.
4) Whatever the professionals say, the days allotted to you are in My hands.

There was no mention of healing at all, unlike with my African illness, when I just knew I wasn't dying. I have, in the privacy of my own prayer times, prayed all the right prayers for healing, nailing every cancer cell to the cross where it belongs. But the verses from Isaiah 57:1-2 come to mind: 'Good people pass away; the godly often die before their time. But no one seems to care or wonder why. No one seems to understand that God is protecting them from the evil to come. For those who follow godly paths will rest in peace when they die.' As I told some old friends at a goodbye party – I won't be here to see it when ISIS takes over Galloway!

The fact is, every person and every Christian will face death at some point, until the Lord returns. Sometimes the Lord will choose to add to our days, but there will come for each of us an illness, an accident, a trauma that He will not heal on this earth. As I had entrusted Aunt Nan's time into His hands, so I did with myself.

Because of metastatic cancer in the brain, I was obliged to give up my driving licence and couldn't carry on with work. However, Margaret was trained and positioned to take over in a way that she hadn't anticipated, and maybe wouldn't have had the confidence to put herself forward for. We had worked hard over the previous weeks getting everything in the office in order. God had planned that the CAP office would have the best person in place at the right time. It was tempting to put the lovely VW that Dad had given me into the workshop at Norheim and sit out the two years until I might get my licence back – it's a force of habit to hold on to our assets. However, God spoke to me, and as it was obvious that Margaret needed a good car to do the CAP Centre Manager's job without being burdened, it was good that she should have it. I had been out with her husband, Jimmy, a couple of weeks earlier as we helped a CAP client move house. Jimmy is a petrol-head and it was clear too that he loved that VW and so it was right for them to have it and for it to be so well used and looked after.

Why should it sit there of no use to me when it could be a blessing for them?

Many of my fellow Christians seemed to disapprove of my passive stance toward my illness, feeling that I should fight for healing as a right. And 'fight' is a word that is bandied around a great deal by many others concerning cancer, especially in obituaries. 'After a brave fight' is the sort of phrase that, having been through cancer myself, I find so meaningless. How can you fight cancer? You can accept the treatments that may slow it down, and do your best to follow the instructions so you get the best out of it and manage the side effects. You can really focus on, and sift through, the mind-boggling amount of information on current research and new cure-alls to be found online. People trying to be helpful send links for all sorts of cures that work for only a few. But I knew this was my time and felt I should go as peacefully as I could.

Neil had to take time off work as I wasn't supposed to be left alone once I started radiotherapy. Thankfully, he had been expressing a readiness and need to take time out from the rigours of a tough long-term counselling job. The timing was good and he was given a year's sabbatical. Our finances have permitted us to live comfortably without working, to travel and to enjoy life to the full. And to date, by the grace of God and the contribution of modern medical treatment, I have been granted 18 months since the possible three-month prognosis. I like to think we have made the best of the time given. We have done so much, including preparing well for what will inevitably follow.

Other ladies in my situation have admitted to just wanting it all to be over, and this is understandable. I am weary of feeling the side effects of treatment and would not be unhappy to head for eternity with God. Several times recently – as of spring 2016 – I have felt a special connection to Habakkuk 2, 'If the vision of God tarry, wait for it; it will surely come!'

After a major seizure, I was hospitalised and then transferred to St Columba's Hospice in Edinburgh, where I will live out the remainder of my days or, at a push, weeks. I have had a very busy and eventful life and I now feel as if I am finally on a real holiday! I am on a driver containing anti-epilepsy and morphine medications and I am eating exactly what I like – the custard here is wonderful and Neil keeps up a good supply of orange Cadbury éclairs!

There is a last time for everything. I will never leave the hospice building again. I am unable to return home as I need constant supervision and access to more immediate medical care. I cannot speak highly enough about St Columba's Hospice; the doctors, nurses and all members of staff here have been superb with me, making me laugh, joke and smile. But there is also a first time for everything, and I know Whose presence I am about to enter. I have, in essence, regained my peace. I have led my life. I have said my farewells. I am ready for the greatest journey of all. I am sleeping my way to Heaven.

CHAPTER 20

NEIL: LIFE WITH A TOOL WAITRESS

The first time I spoke with Annie was by telephone. I had called her after picking up a leaflet about CAP and wanted to learn more about what her organisation did. On a personal level, I was concerned about credit card debt which was showing signs of spiralling out of control; and on a professional level, in my role as an alcohol counsellor, I wanted to see if CAP might be able to support some of my clients who were seriously in debt, sometimes to the tune of many thousands of pounds.

There was something about Annie's voice that really appealed to me. She was obviously intelligent and spoke very clearly, but there was also reassurance in her words and in her tone that struck me immediately. We met at my home and physically she looked attractive to me, but it was her voice, eyes and personality that bowled me over. Somewhat jaundiced by previous relationships, I felt that Annie offered something fresh. That something was a searing integrity, straightforwardness, an intense warmth and humour, her strong faith, and infectious enthusiasm. Here was someone not out for herself, but inspirational, caring, calm and with that rare ability to make you feel like you were of great value to them. How often do we feel undervalued and uncared for in this world? Too often! Yet for me, here was my new friend who inspired, motivated and cared. My curiosity grew.

As the weeks and months tumbled by, we became firm friends

and would occasionally meet for coffee (tea in Annie's case), or go for a walk in the countryside. The more I learned about her background in Galloway, her unhappiness at Aberdeen University, her conversion to God and her ministry in Africa, the more I liked her, and the more time I wanted to spend with her. I was a tad disappointed to learn that she was dating another guy at the time; but I was careful (or so I thought!) not to show my growing love for this remarkable woman. Annie sensed what was happening in me and she did reassure me that the feelings were reciprocated, but she was hugely honourable and did care a lot for the man she was seeing, so I promised not to interfere. We both behaved well – and I admired how Annie handled the situation. She did not lead me on or make false promises, and I responded by keeping my distance, not enquiring too deeply about her private life.

On Valentine's Day 2011, whilst out walking in the foothills of the Pentland Hills, I could contain my curiosity no further and I enquired as to her 'eligibility'. She explained to me that, whilst she still hoped to retain a friendship with the chap she had being seeing until recently, she was single and free to see whoever she wanted. Amazingly, she wanted to see me. That very day we became a couple. I was overjoyed. It felt right – and it was. Five days later we were engaged. Four weeks later we were married.

Why the haste? Importantly, we both sensed that it was right. We had both enjoyed (and endured on occasion) a number of relationships, but neither of us had previously felt this certain sense that we were simply meant to be together. It wasn't just down to the fact that we had the Galloway connection, it was something that went way beyond words. It was love; a love that has never left me, only strengthened. The other reason for a fast wedding was because Annie knew her father was dying of brain tumours and may only have had weeks to live. She was determined that he should attend our wedding in Stranraer, and that was what he did. He had a very happy day and was one of the very last to leave the reception. Requesting Billy's permission to marry his lovely daughter was more of a challenge for me than the wedding itself. I had travelled down to Norheim, the family home, to see him and also to meet Annie's mother Margaret for the first time. I had the temerity to arrive five minutes late and this was considered to be a black mark against my name for a family that adhered to strict and rigid schedules!

Actually, I was to get on well with Billy and I was relieved that he lived for several more months so that I was able to more fully know him. I recall how proud he looked when he presented me with his fully kilted outfit (Lindsay tartan) and I felt a real sense that he was accepting me into his family. I am now the proud owner of Billy's (and John Noakes') Blue Peter badge.

The marriage itself had been a happy day not just for Billy, but for all present. Annie looked particularly beautiful in her favourite African outfit, which was something rarely seen in Stranraer and caused a gentle stir. Only family members were present at the wedding, as Annie and I had resolved to hold a much larger celebration for friends at a later date.

Neither of us had ever been married before, so there was a real novelty and adventurous side to what lay ahead. We were both working and had our own friends, interests, hobbies and families to incorporate into our new dual existence. I returned to church with Annie for the first time in years (having previously drifted away due to a sense of disappointment and disillusionment) and I found myself enjoying it more this time around, not least because I could stand and hold Annie's hand and listen to her gorgeous and sincere singing voice belting out the hymns. Annie also encouraged me to attend the monthly Swahili service she helped to conduct. The warmth of the people there, the welcome they afforded all attendees, and the uplifting rhythm and vibrancy and sheer enthusiasm that they introduced to their services was unlike anything I had experienced before. Singing songs in Swahili was another first and unforgettable event.

In return for Annie introducing me to her Christian family, I invited her along to the odd football match and punk concert.

I can recall that first gig and my feeling of slight concern that she may not take to a band called 'The Damned'. When we arrived at the crowded venue, with perhaps a couple of thousand others, I deliberately ensured that we stayed near the back with my ageing punk friends in case anything offended Annie's sensibilities. I need not have worried. Halfway through the concert she grabbed my hand and led me forward all the way to the front row where she pogoed with the best of them, all with a smile on her face!

Before we had married, Annie had asked me what remained undone in my life and what I dreamed of doing. I explained that my life had already been quite full – professionally I had experienced a number of roles, including around 15 years in total as a bereavement, generic and alcohol counsellor. I enjoyed being a tour guide in my beloved Edinburgh, I had relished sports in my youth, particularly cross country and marathon running before a long bout of ill health put an end to it (like Annie, I had suffered from ME), I had had a number of relationships, a great family, many hobbies including writing poetry (really living on the edge!), and I knew where my politics lay. I had had adventures and known good times and bad; and so what could be left?

I thought about her question and stated that we were probably a tad old to start a family, although I would love us to have a dog someday when we were less busy. However, I would like to learn more about flora and fauna and birdlife (I knew that Annie excelled in this!), learn a few words in Swahili, which she spoke so competently, and understand more about her incredibly powerful relationship with God. Oh – and travel a bit.

Annie did indeed help me learn the name of some flowers and birds, taught me about country life, and helped my faltering DIY skills (hers were far superior to mine, not least because of her upbringing with the ever practical and creative Billy and her aircraft mechanic background) and we often talked of her faith and how she came to God. Sometimes I was envious that she seemed to have a direct link, whereas my relationship was more fuzzy, sceptical at times. I wished that I had her overwhelming trust and crystal-clear faith, which was never in doubt.

Whereas I had thought that our conversation about 'things I'd dreamt of doing' was one of those casual fantasy lists that we occasionally drift towards, I'd reckoned without the Annie Factor. She had listened carefully to me and rose to the challenge. Never more so than when it came to travelling! Our official honeymoon was in Rome, but then others followed thick and fast. Thankfully we had understanding families, as over the course of the following five years we were to have many, many more honeymoons including Lithuania, Mediterranean cruises, Iceland, Paris, Berlin, Prague, Amsterdam, a boat trip down the Danube, and a trip across the USA by train.

From these trips so many adventures accrued that are etched upon my memory and in my heart forever. These would include our health spa trip in Lithuania where one of the 'treatments' involved sitting together in a heart-shaped jacuzzi, surrounded by candles, incense and uninspiring Eastern European love songs before a rather stern Russian member of staff instructed us in no uncertain terms to 'relax and make love'. The tears rolled down our cheeks as soon as she had left us to ourselves.

The sheer rugged beauty of Iceland mesmerised us, as did the raw shark meat we ate. In Romania, we spent an evening 7,000 feet up in the Carpathian Mountains. After our meal in the 'Ice Hotel', which we ate whilst wearing at least four layers of clothing (and discovered that eating with knives and forks whilst wearing thick gloves is no mean feat), we retired to what is claimed to be the highest igloo in the world and attempted to sleep on our beds made out of ice but covered in animal skins. The temperature *inside* our igloo dropped below minus 20 degrees Celsius and considerable amounts of vodka were consumed.

In Amsterdam, we found ourselves in the Red Light district. Annie asked me to stand by a canal edge so she could take a photograph of me. She said, 'Ha! You'll never guess what I have shot as the backdrop of my picture of you – it's a replica of the Moulin Rouge that we saw in Paris.'

'Ha,' I retorted, 'you'll never guess what's been happening behind your back while you were taking your picture.'

Annie turned round to find a young lady in a shop window dressed in about half a bikini beckoning my way! We giggled like children and moved on.

Travelling around America – largely by train – was another unforgettable experience. The trigger for this trip was a most extraordinary event. The immortal Auntie Caroline, who had hardly dated in her life, was getting married aged 73 to an 86-year-old gentleman. We attended the wedding, where Annie participated in Tanzanian wedding customs to solemnise the proceedings. A few months later, Caroline and her husband Bill formally adopted Bill's 56-year-old former foster daughter.

After the wedding, we went 'rail about' on the famous Amtrak system. Here, the adventure really began. On one occasion, we took a boat trip deep into the swamplands of Louisiana and our tour guide produced a surprise gift for us all: a baby alligator which he had muzzled to prevent him from snapping. Annie later chastised him as she was concerned for the animal's wellbeing… but not before all on the boat had had an opportunity to hold the creature and handle him. By the time the poor beast reached Annie he was clearly fed up and lashed out with his tail, firmly whacking Annie in the face. Our tour guide was full of remorse and concern for Annie's wellbeing, but she quickly re-assured him: 'Don't be daft. I'm fine. I've spent many years in Africa AND I'm a farmer's daughter from Galloway!'

Away from the exotic travels, though, many other adventures were to be had. We took a hot air balloon ride over the Pentland Hills to the south of Edinburgh. We lifted off at dawn through great swathes of clouds. I loved the experience of soaring higher and higher, but I noticed that Annie was looking a little less self-assured than usual; and it was then that she confessed to me that she had a fear of heights! I was amazed. A woman who had done all that she had done so fearlessly, including taking flying lessons to be an aircraft pilot, was trembling as we arched our way over the hills. I asked her the obvious question as to why on earth she had agreed to go hot air ballooning with me and she said simply, 'Because I love being with you!' That was my Annie. I could have wept. As the balloon steadied itself and we reached beyond the clouds and felt as if we were within touching distance of the velvet blue sky, we both relaxed and just enjoyed the panoramic views, the silence, the wonder of it all. Surreally, after a slightly bumpy landing, we ended up being served champagne in a field by Lord Torphichen of West Lothian.

Of all the trips that we were fortunate enough to make together, though, the one that had the greatest impact upon me, perhaps inevitably, was our visit to East Africa. The adventures we had there, the people we met, the Mkumi wildlife park where we both contracted malaria and were almost attacked by a female elephant protecting her young, were nothing in comparison to my utter respect and pride and joy at seeing Annie in her beloved 'home'. Ever since I had become acquainted with Annie, it was obvious that she had a great love for Africa and that she was keen to return. When I agreed to accompany her, it was with a degree of trepidation – I wasn't sure how I would fare there and Annie was also a tad concerned that I might somehow embarrass her! As things transpired, she told me upon our return home that she was very proud of how I had behaved, of the sensitivity and patience and respect that I had shown to all those that we had met and interacted with. It was tremendously high praise from her and I was grateful.

It was I, however, who had the real reason to be proud – of Annie. With her flawless Swahili, her full understanding of the quirks and the customary ways of being and behaving in Tanzania, she was utterly comfortable and joyous wherever she went. The locals showed her the same great respect that she showed to them. She was calm, polite, humorous, and assertive when she had to be and, above all, she was so obviously happy to be there. It was slowly dawning on me just how African Annie was; in thought, in heart, in dress, in life. Annie encouraged me to join her at her local church in Dodoma. However, after four hours of standing in my kilt regalia in the blistering heat listening to the young female preacher shouting at us in animated Swahili, I had to step outside.

Of course, our marriage wasn't all about travel, it was also about everyday routines; tending to our work, socialising with friends and family, indulging in hobbies, housework and gardening as well as visiting her parents' home in Galloway, and then, after Billy's death, finding Margaret a new home in Edinburgh.

Although on many levels it had been so simple, I think it took me and Annie a little time to settle *fully* into the rhythm of married life. We were both strongly independent people, and, although we had many similarities in our make-up, we also could see the world differently. I believe that this is normal! We adapted – my family and friends quickly became Annie's too. Her family and friends became mine. We shared interests, working out which movies we enjoyed together, which ones to avoid. We went to the theatre, cinema, football, concerts. We walked together and often had friends (and their dogs) come visit. We went to church together. Annie even used to join me when I undertook work as a tour guide in Edinburgh. The tours, the walks, the movies, always felt better when I was holding hands with Annie.

Annie's African connections ensured that we had considerable contact with this community in Edinburgh and beyond. On one occasion, we were invited to attend an event at which the Tanzanian Ambassador to the UK would be present. I recall sitting at our dining table, eager to try out my 18 words of Swahili on the guy next to me. A few minutes in, he took my hand and said, 'It is very nice that you are speaking Swahili to me, but I am a Nigerian and I do not understand a word that you are saying. English, please!' I had learned another valuable lesson: never assume!

I had a cursory glance at the dance floor and saw many people swaying around the room in Conga formation. This was my chance to get up there with Annie. She had bossed me into re-learning Scottish country dance music and learning a little Swahili. Now was my chance to be with her on an 'African' dance floor. But where *was* she? I glanced around all the tables. No sign. Then I looked more closely at the noisy dance floor and realised she was leading the Conga line. I just sat back and grinned and applauded her. What a woman, what an amazing wife!

We had promised, ever since our 'shotgun' wedding, that we would hold a much larger celebration, in due course, where many more family members and friends could be present. It took us two years before we found the time to settle on a venue and a programme. The event was held in Dunfermline in Fife, Scotland, in a municipal building which was large enough to host the 300 people who rolled up. We had a renewal of vows with the same minister who had married us, speeches, a banquet, helium balloons, a ceilidh, African music, a disco, and finally a stunning firework display on the lawns. The whole event lasted around seven hours, but few went home early that night. I was told later that the fireworks were seen by friends of ours back in Edinburgh. More importantly, many contacted us later to say it was the best party they had ever experienced. I was pleased for them, but above all, I was pleased for Annie. The meticulous planning that we had poured ourselves into had paid off.

Above all, though, it was how Annie was with *people* that never ceased to amaze me. She had that very rare gift of being able to put someone at their ease, instantly showing a genuine interest in that person and, with her twinkling warm eyes and her heart-melting smile, within a few minutes she could and did let that person know that they were valued, even loved. You had to spend only a little time in Annie's company to see her 'aura' at work – it was indescribable. Partly it was her strength of personality; partly it was down to her great faith in God.

I can recall on our return from Rome losing track of Annie in the cluttered airport. I finally found her chatting to a handsome Italian security guard. Their conversation dragged on and on to the extent that I was concerned that we would miss our flight home. Eventually Annie came over to me and explained that 'the man just needed to be listened to'. I got it, said no more and rushed her through to the departure lounge. I never once felt I had reason to be jealous when she spent time with any man – this type of encounter was simply indicative of her overflowing love for everyone around her, and the way she'd handled the situation with the man she was seeing when we were first getting to know each other had showed me that she was too concerned for the honour of all concerned to engage in even the mildest flirtation.

One evening I returned home about midnight after a punk concert. Annie was in bed asleep when my phone went. It was a friend I had been with at the gig; he had lost his keys and couldn't get home from a deserted railway station. I groaned. I couldn't rescue him as I wasn't fit to drive after a couple of beers. Within seconds Annie had worked out what was going on, slipped on a dressing gown and headed off to collect Dave from the railway station to bring him back and spend the night in our home. No need to think about it; this was Annie's spontaneous reaction at work!

It wasn't just people who benefited from Annie's presence. Her love of animals (especially dogs) was legendary. One Saturday afternoon, whilst pushing our way through crowds on Edinburgh's Princes Street, she suddenly stopped and knelt down to pat a poodle. Apparently oblivious to the commotion around her, she eventually stood up, thanked the dog's owner for 'sharing her dog with us', and moved on, explaining to me in hushed tones that the dog needed to say hello to her.

This picture that I am seeking to paint of my life with a 'tool waitress' is how things were for the first three years of marriage with Annie. We were happy, at peace, in love and forging a unique partnership. As a friend shrewdly pointed out to me recently, together we were greater than the sum of our parts. We were so fortunate to have sufficient funds to be comfortable, we enjoyed our work, our friendships and our families, we could afford to be generous with others, and Annie was a giver. As part of her faith she insisted that we give away 10% of all we earned or had inherited. It was frequently a much higher percentage than this. Sometimes it was money that was gifted, sometimes a car, sometimes flowers. Whatever was gifted, Annie always did so with *love*.

The word that we came to use frequently to describe our first few years of marriage was 'carefree'. I don't think we ever took this state of being for granted, but we did come to cherish our carefree moments more and more when black clouds descended – when in May 2014 Annie was diagnosed with breast cancer.

Initially, we took it in our stride, as we were reassured that she may have another ten, even 20 years of life. However, further tests showed that the cancer had spread to her lungs and her liver. Finally, we were advised that cancer had been found in her brain.

She may, they said, only have three months to live.

I remember this consultation vividly. She took in the information measuredly and calmly. One of the medical team apologised to Annie that another colleague couldn't be present to offer more details, but he was off sick. Annie leaned across earnestly and said, 'I hope he's going to be ok?' There she was, checking on another person's welfare within a few minutes of being told that she was going to die shortly. Only Annie!

Tears were something that Annie and I rarely shared. I had seen her upset on a couple of occasions. Mea culpa (translated: my fault)! I was guilty of pushing her too far on occasion and her frustration would cause her upset, and I can remember twice in our marriage feeling very guilty that I had pushed Annie to tears – tears of exasperation with her husband! The only other time I had seen Annie cry was when she talked about dogs that she had owned, but who had either died or she had had to leave behind. Her Rhodesian Ridgeback, Bracken, brought out emotions in Annie that she seldom expressed for the human beings that she loved so much.

However, immediately after that last, most shocking diagnosis at the Western General hospital in Edinburgh, I drove her to Dobbies Garden Centre on the outskirts of town, where we sipped tea and watched ducks play in a little pond, our eyes moist as we reflected upon the enormity of what we had just been told. It was sinking in fast. Annie only had a few months to live and we had just moved her mother to Edinburgh to be closer to the cherished daughter whom she relied on so heavily!

Following Annie's lead, we didn't dwell too long upon our emotions (an anathema for me as a counsellor – it seemed to go against the grain!) and we crashed straight into Lawson Mode: PRACTICALITIES. We had to break the news in person to Margaret and my parents, to other family members and friends, telephone around, set up round robin e-mails, inform employers that we needed time out (eventually pulling away from work altogether), we had paperwork to attend to, the two homes to think about as well as two further apartments in Tanzania needing to be sold and lawyers to communicate with. The list was seemingly endless. Yet, wisely, we also set time aside for ourselves to talk, laugh, emote, howl at the moon.

Seemingly endless bouts of medical meetings and treatments followed. Annie agreed to undertake radiotherapy and then chemotherapy, saw her GP regularly, and joined a Women's Cancer Support group. We visited 'Maggie's Centre', Macmillan nurses, and sought out support regarding what welfare benefits we could claim. Annie lost her hair; we purchased wigs. She got more fatigued; we stayed in more and read and watched TV. She began writing her life story. We went to Norheim and appointed a gardener there and decluttered. We visited her family members and friends and mine, seeking to reassure them that all was as good as it could be… given the circumstances. On and on and on it went. *That* was key. It *did* go on… and

Annie was granted almost two and a half years from her initial diagnosis to when she passed away, far longer than we had anticipated. This was a truly precious gift.

This additional time was used very wisely as it felt to us like a fragile, rare jewel to be handled with great care and respect. Annie explained to me that she had not heard God promising her a healing miracle this time around. Rather she had heard that *'nothing must be allowed to disturb her peace'*. She looked at me rather markedly when she delivered this thought! The penny was dropping for me that whilst I, and Annie's loved ones and friends, were largely grappling around for treatment options both allopathic and complementary, Annie herself was ready to depart. She had the utmost hope, total faith that she would be 'going to glory', so why hang about Planet Earth feeling sick and tired if she could reach Heaven?

Having dealt with many practicalities and put things in order, I asked Annie what more she needed or wanted to do with the time afforded to her, to us. She wanted to visit her friends in Galloway and her church friends and others in different parts of England, including staying with, and spending time with, her two cousins who lived in London. She wrote notes to her immediate family (and mine) thanking each one individually for the impact they had had on her life. She gifted jewellery, cars, a grandfather clock and bric-a-brac to friends, family and charity shops. We gardened, we went out for coffee, and we walked. Every bird, every flower, every wave, every sunset took on more significance than before.

Whilst contending with all that was occurring to us and around us, another thunderbolt struck. Upon visiting Annie's mother, we discovered her body in her flat. She had died just minutes before we had reached her. A frantic hour or two passed with the caretaker of the building, ambulance men, policemen and women (this was an 'unexplained death', after all, and we were gently but carefully questioned), and finally Margaret's GP buzzing around the flat. After they had all been and gone, and we had the reassurance that my mother-in-law had died painlessly and instantaneously of a heart attack, I slumped back in a chair, wondering what on earth was going through Annie's mind. First her father, now her mother, whom we had taken to Edinburgh Zoo to see the meerkats only days previously. Annie was sitting quietly with her comforting mug of tea in hand and finally said: 'Well, this has been a good day.'

'What?!' I squealed.

'Yes; Mum has gone before me. She doesn't have to worry about me anymore. She is at peace. It's a blessing.'

Annie loved her mother dearly and had cared for her devoutly, but her mind was in a different sphere from most of us mere mortals. While I was showing emotion, she was showing calm and logical thinking.

Importantly for Annie, she was getting the opportunity to fulfil her wishes, to live her remaining dreams. This included the trip to America where she attended Auntie Caroline's wedding celebration in Florida, before we travelled around half the United States by train.

Despite some discomfort and fatigue from the seemingly endless bouts of chemotherapy and the constant meetings with consultants, generally Annie's health had been reasonable. I think she endured the chemo more for my sake than for her own. She was functioning independently. She was strong, determined, and as mischievous as ever, with plans, goals and lists keeping her – and me! – fully occupied. We even learned how to complete the odd crossword and game of Sudoku. She planned Christmas 2014 meticulously, inviting all of my family to spend the day with us. Annie had her preparations down to a fine art and it was one of the happiest family gatherings that we had ever enjoyed together.

Two days later, calamity struck. Annie had the first of many seizures. The cancer was wreaking havoc in her brain. Watching her writhing in such discomfort was traumatising for me. How much more horrific for her? The initial ambulance first went to the wrong house, then pronounced her OK. It departed. The next bout of seizures began barely an hour later and eventually she was hospitalised. This was the start of one of the toughest times in Annie's life and in our marriage. Any semblance of remaining carefree had gone. We had to cancel our annual New Year's trip with friends, where Annie had spent the last seven Hogmanays. We could no longer plan ahead and we knew that Annie's health was declining constantly and irrevocably. There was nothing more that Annie or I or the medics, or anyone else, could do but wait and pray.

Annie reminded me that she had just one more aspiration, which was to write her memoirs. She was at peace within herself and did not want that peace disturbed. She was more than ready to meet her Maker. She told me that she would miss me greatly, that she was sorry to be leaving her family and friends and even the cats, birds and squirrels that she had befriended in our garden (!), but that she WAS ready to depart, and that she had something much bigger, better, and brighter to look forward to once she had left the troubles and travails of Earth behind.

Although she was still very calm at a deep level, and her faith was giving her huge comfort emotionally, her mind was still very active. She insisted that she carry on with her writings, and we arranged for a number of her African artefacts to be bequeathed to the National Museum of Scotland in Edinburgh, where they shall be exhibited in their full glory someday with a plaque detailing the possessions and their original owner. We also arranged to sponsor an acre of semi-ancient woodland in rural Galloway with 'our' park bench in a prominent position, to celebrate our five years of marriage. It reads simply:

Margaret Anne Lawson and Neil Dickson Conn
Five Golden Years
Much too Short
From Here to Eternity
2011–2016

It was time for Annie to withdraw a little more from 'public life'. Her final few services pastoring the Swahili group were particularly touching. Despite her infirmity, she led discussions on such weighty topics as the meaning of the Ten Commandments!

Annie knew that she was retreating from the outside world a little, as she needed to rest up. There was always a concern that she would have further seizures. I think I dreaded them more than she did. She was still willing to travel independently, but I was anxious that she would collapse in a chaotic, public environment and I felt that Annie needed and deserved better than that.

A friend of mine, Innes, whom Annie had grown very fond of, was travelling from his home in the States to walk the second half of his epic journey along what is known as the Scottish National Trail in June 2016. Originally, I had offered to travel and collect him from his final destination of Cape Wrath in the far northwest of Scotland. Far from dissuading me from travelling, Annie insisted that I go – and that she go too. Once she had made her mind up, there was no point arguing with this lady. And her mind *was* made up!

With hindsight, I am so grateful that we made what turned out to be our final substantial journey together. Not only was it wonderful spending time with my friend Innes and our buddy David who had also walked some of the Trail, but it was so good to spend time travelling through our own magnificent country. Annie and I had spent so much time journeying around Europe and Africa and America that we had somehow managed to neglect our own backyard, with its adorable scenery and rich and diverse history. This oversight was erased with a single trip!

Not long after our return, with all I's dotted and T's crossed and with Annie having pronounced that she now felt she could go in peace, she had a further seizure. Hospitalised once more, she discovered that she had lost much of the movement on the left-hand side of her body. In addition to facing terminal cancer, she now also faced with what would have been a permanent disability. She had had enough. She wanted out.

Annie, the medics and I all concurred that it would not be right to send Annie home. St Columba's Hospice in Edinburgh was to be her final port of call in this world. She was not coming home to me and my heart ached.

Within 48 hours of being admitted to St Columba's, Annie told me that her peace was being disturbed. I had recently cajoled her into trying a remedy that claimed to stop cancer in its tracks. In addition, I had encouraged her to take mistletoe injections, which may have prolonged her life. Annie said she was unhappy continuing with the remedies. Rightly, she pointed out to me that, even if her cancer was held at bay, she still had the issue of a lack of movement on the left side of her body to contend with and she did not want to spend the rest of her days reliant upon others for feeding her, dressing her, showering her. I got it. I did not want to disturb her peace. Annie's wishes were paramount. Her voice, her individuality and her dignity usurped all other considerations. Thank God she had Him in her life; this gave her such peace and that in turn kept me sane.

I found it hard explaining to people who wanted to call her, visit her, and text her that this would not be possible. Some folks who loved and cared so much for Annie were keen to communicate directly with her, but she was adamant that this would not be appropriate. She was exhausted, needed to sleep a great deal and, crucially, wanted to be remembered for the person that she really was, rather than a more vulnerable individual preparing to depart the world. She needed peace.

The staff at St Columba's were superb; each and every one of them brought her laughter and love and she reciprocated, in spades. It was a matter of huge relief to us that we both knew that Annie had found the right place to die. 'Co-incidence, or God-incidence?' Annie would ask me with a grin.

She asked me to write a poem entitled 'Forget Me Not', which is the emblem of St Columba's. I misinterpreted her meaning initially, thinking that she wanted me to compose a poem to help ensure that she was remembered after she was gone. Oh, no – it wasn't that at all! It was Annie asking me to put into poetry her sincere thanks to all those at St Columba's who were ensuring her end of life was as loving, compassionate and honourable as was humanly possible. The poem reads:

FORGET ME NOT
The 'forget me not' is so much more than just a flower
It is not here just to remember those who have lost their lives to cancer
And who have memorials in their name

It is to remind us of all the staff here
Who work so hard and with such compassion
Those who smile and laugh here in the face of death and rain

The blonde bombshells and dark-haired nurses
Who toil gently here with such good grace
With sincerity, kindness and inexhaustible compassion

Their ethos: one of such high standards and warmth and mirth
Paying such close attention to every aspect of love and care
No cynicism, no grudging – yet always there for us with joyous passion

So by all means 'forget me not' when our time is spent
And remember all those yet to come to find release

But above all celebrate with gratitude and heartfelt thanks
The people here who make our time here one of peace.

Not for the first time in my life, nor the last, I was blown away by the fact that my gorgeous wife was thinking of others. But at this time of *all* times?

Weeks passed. I travelled in from home each day to spend hours at Annie's bedside. We relaxed the 'no visitors' rule a little to ensure that Annie had Communion with some close friends. We invited Dayspring MacLeod, who helped write this book, to visit her three times to get a real sense of who Annie was, and begin to grasp the extraordinary life that she had led.

In Annie's final days, she asked if two of her closest friends – Evelyn and Sue – who had a medical background could attend her, to support her if required. Those final few days in August 2016 were no Sunday School picnic for Annie herself and we knew that the end was nigh. She was experiencing more discomfort and was dozing in and out of consciousness.

I had determined that the time was right for me to stay overnight at St Columba's. The very first evening I was there, a Sunday, the nurse on duty advised me that Annie may be ready to pass. I sat by her bedside, went for a rest and then returned. It was obvious that she was going. I was almost willing it on – for her sake, not for mine.

As I have alluded to, my conviction, any faith I have, is not in the same league as Annie's. Whilst I have doubts, she had none. Therefore, out of love, out of respect for her, I did that night what felt right. I read her passages from a novel of faith, I ensured she grasped a 'holding cross' which one of the kindly pastors at St Columba's had offered her weeks before and I got down on bended knee and I recited the Lord's Prayer to her. All the time the lyrics of a song by my favourite band (The Cure) rattled round my head: 'There's nothing left but faith.' She opened her eyes a little – there was love there – and she smiled a little, and then breathed her last. A nurse was with me, stroking her hair and holding her hand. Annie had passed. In peace.

* * *

Now, as I reflect upon my life with my 'Tool Waitress', several more thunderbolts have hit me hard:

She taught me so much. Not least how to love again.

Through her I did not receive all the answers regarding my constant battle with faith, but one of the most important things I learned is the need to differentiate between organised religions (which can be a source of real good, but sometimes are twisted badly by egos, politics, and power-hungry souls) and faith. Faith in God is always good.

She taught me how to be a little better in the world (not perfect!), to show a little more tolerance, patience, to step back and think a little more, say a little less.

Annie was immensely practical and I have learned to be more patient with projects, to swallow pride and cry out for help when needed!

The vast outpouring of grief, memories and emotions that Annie has engendered in so many people in different regions across the globe have reminded me how widely loved and respected she was. She is being missed and I am so immensely proud of my wife and what she achieved.

The one message above all others that I continue to hold dear is that Annie would not wish me to spend the remainder of my days crying into my coffee/beer about how much I miss her, how much it hurts now that she's gone (and I confess that it does hurt), but rather to get on with the process of life, to accommodate her loss into my life and to *celebrate* all that she gave me. To learn from her, to be inspired by her example, to laugh with her again. 'Carpe diem' ('Seize the Day') was one of our favourite clichés, but clichés are often there for a good reason. I hope that you, too, can seize the day.

After all, it's what Annie would have wanted.

NEIL CONN. ON BEHALF OF MY BELOVED WIFE, ANNIE. RIP.

CHAPTER 21

THE BRIDGE

Margaret Anne Lawson passed into the Lord's presence on 22 August 2016. Being particularly loved, she ended up with no fewer than four funerals and memorial services, including one in her beloved Tanzania. She requested that the following story be printed and given to the guests at her 'official' funeral. It's a striking instance of African life.

We came to a crossroads where we could choose a long route that we knew to be a good road, or a shortcut that was more uncertain. There was some disagreement as to whether the shortcut was passable, and after praying for guidance, the Christians in the car came to the decision that we should go for the shorter route.

Contrary to our concerns, it was a very good road – as good as tarmac, which is most unusual in rural Tanzania – and that confirmed us in our supposition that it was indeed passable. We enjoyed our journey, until we came across a fishing boat sitting in the middle of the road! We soon realised that the bridge across the river was out. The lights of the city were tantalizingly close, but without the bridge, there was no way to our destination.

As we retraced our journey, we discussed what God wanted us to learn from our mistake. We came to realise three things:

- *No matter how good or how enjoyable the road is, it is of no value at all if it doesn't go to the destination.*
- *Cars had passed us going in the other direction, and must have known the bridge was out, but nobody stopped to warn us.*
- *We were so confident of ourselves that we never thought to ask.*

Annie wished to share this story as her dearest friends gather to say their last farewells. There is a Bridge, one on which she built her life and put her entire trust. Your road may be smooth and pleasant, but what is your destination? Jesus Christ is the one road to eternal life. He gave His life as a sacrifice for all who will come to Him, and rose again to show His victory over death so that all who believe may also live forever with Him.

Annie knew Jesus well, and trusted Him to hold her life secure in His keeping. She was fond of saying in the midst of a dangerous situation, 'the safest place to be is in the eye of God's will,' and Annie reminded her friends of this, even from her bed in the hospice. This knowledge gave her great peace in life and a certain future. She is now not only in Jesus' will, but in His arms.

If you don't know Annie's Bridge, she urges you to meet Him in the pages of the Bible, His great love letter to the people He created.

'Come to me, all who are weary and burdened,
and I will give you rest.' – Matt. 11:28

ACKNOWLEDGEMENTS

This story of a remarkable life, conceived and written by Annie herself, became a three-way collaboration when she realised in summer 2016 that she would be unable to bring the book to completion. Upon her passing, it was lovingly nurtured to fruition by her husband Neil Conn, with supplementary materials collected and edited by Dayspring MacLeod.

There was a great deal of help and support in producing the final manuscript, and Neil would like to express a debt of gratitude to those who made it possible.

Firstly, to those who enriched Annie's final years and months: The congregation of Holy Trinity Church, Wester Hailes, in the Southwest area of Edinburgh, Scotland; Annie's final home church, which has provided emotional support to Neil and hosted a standing-room-only celebration service of Annie's life. HTC's retired minister, Rev. Kenny Borthwick, who married Neil and Annie, and who also renewed their vows. Current minister Rev. Ian Macdonald, who conducted Annie's funeral service and supported her in her role at CAP (Christians Against Poverty) as a debt counsellor; Margaret Farquhar, who was a great help in Annie's final months at work and took over her job at CAP.

Inexpressible thanks also go to all at the Western General Hospital (Edinburgh) and also the staff and chaplaincy at St Columba's Hospice, who cared for Annie with dignity, humour and great kindness in her final weeks. Annie's family, the Sproat Clan, consisting of Annie's cousins and their families, and Neil's family members and friends, including brother Magnus and sisters Alison and Morag, who all showed great love and concern for Annie throughout her illness. Finally, of great help to Neil were Sue Begg, Mike & Evelyn Banks and Angie Thomson, who participated in Annie's final communion service at the hospice.

Much appreciation is due to the staff and management at Mission Aviation Fellowship, where Annie was remembered as a seminal character. Stories, articles, advice, and many more services were rendered by Andy Martin, Ruth Box, Chris Lukkien, and Ruth Whitaker.

Of great importance to Annie during her married life was the staff of DARF (Dignity Alert and Research Forum), including Dr Monica Elias Magoke-Mhoja and her family, who became Annie's 'Tanzanian family' in Scotland. DARF is a charity that Annie was involved with, highlighting the issue of female genital mutilation in Scotland. Dr Magoke-Mhoja has been helpful in providing information for this book and by leading a moving Swahili service of thanksgiving for Annie's life, as well as supporting Neil through his bereavement. Her daughters, Esther and Jessica, have also produced beautiful tributes to Annie.

Besides those already mentioned above, Dayspring MacLeod would like to express thanks to many of Annie's friends who provided interviews, emails, photos, and other materials for the book: Alice Hew, 'Auntie' Caroline Ackerman Marschall, Carol McCusker, Kim Bower, Andrew Fothergill, Morag Taylor, Morag Bryce, Elizabeth Taylor, Angela Wilson, Ruth McKelvey, Julie & Chris Demetriou (with Lily the Dog), and Carol Brown. Annie's 'fan club' at Old Luce Parish Church, Glenluce, Scotland, were instrumental in preserving many of her thoughts and anecdotes through a collection of her newsletters and correspondence. Irene Howat, who included Annie in her book 'Ten Girls Who Used Their Talents,' introduced Dayspring to Neil and Annie and made the collaboration possible. She and Karen Murdurasi have also been helpful and reliable beta readers.

Finally, thank you to Richard Roper of RoperPenberthy Publishing and David Powell of Freedom Publishing, whose enthusiasm for this book was immediate and deeply refreshing, and who has been a most helpful guide and facilitator in bringing Annie's singular story to life.